Jill Oxton's

Beautiful Beading

for beginners

and beyond

FINDING NYMO - PAGE 57

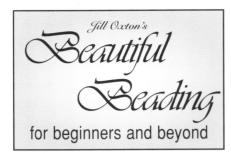

Jill Oxton's

Beautiful Beading

for beginners and beyond

Editor
JILL OXTON

Designers
ERIKA BANNA
MARGARET LEYLAND
MARY MOTT
DI NOYCE
GWENDOLYN OXTON
JILL OXTON

Proof Reader
GABRIELLE CANNY

Distribution Enquiries
WENDY WILSON
wendy@jilloxtonxstitch.com

Photography
BLINK PRODUCTIONS

Reprographics
COLORWIZE, South Australia

Printed in Hong Kong

ISBN 0-9587576-2-3

Jill Oxton's Cross Stitch & Beading
is published quarterly in January, April, July and October by

JILL OXTON PUBLICATIONS PTY LTD
PO Box 283, Park Holme,
South Australia 5043
PH within Aust: (08) 8276 2722
PH outside Aust: +61 8 8276 2722
FAX: (08) 8374 3494
EMAIL: jill@jilloxtonxstitch.com
WEB: www.jilloxtonxstitch.com

Contents

Instructions

The Projects

Introduction

*Pic right:
Bezel Locket,
featured in
Jill Oxtons
Cross Stitch
& Beading
Issue 56, is
worked in
11/0 Japanese
Cylinder
Beads using a
combination
of square
stitch and
brick stitch.*

Our aim in collecting together projects for this book was to give you useful items to make while learning (and mastering) the construction methods and many of the items we have made can also be adapted to other designs.

Being very 'hands on', we can only talk with authority about materials, stitches and beads that we have personally used, and this is what we have done here.

Square stitch is the stitch I find I most commonly use. We have gone into depth with this stitch, introducing other stitches for trimmings, chains, bases and embellishments.

Included are detailed instructions on square stitch, taking you step by step with the projects in this book, from the simple to the more complex.

As a designer of tapestry and cross stitch for many years, I discovered square stitch and loom work lent themselves perfectly to charted designs. I do not like working on frames and as my loom work is less than perfect, square stitch has become my stitch of choice. It has a nice rhythm to it and I find it very relaxing.

Square stitch also has a lot of other advantages.

1.You need minimal equipment, basically consisting of needles, scissors and needle-nose pliers for attaching findings (and even these are the ridged pliers 'borrowed' from the family toolbox).

2. It is very portable.

3. It is a strong stitch and ends are woven in as you go, so the piece doesn't need a lot of finishing, other than findings, fringes and straps.

4. Square stitch adapts itself to different tensions. I believe our tension is our tension and there is not a lot we can do about it, except learn how to adapt the stitch to suit yourself and relax and enjoy working it.

It helps to remember that the beauty of something handmade is in its imperfections and the love put into it. Practice makes perfect and sometimes you just have to experiment.

We recommend that beginners to square stitch start with a bracelet. By the time you have made this you should have mastered square stitch. When this comes automatically, you are ready to go onto pieces that involve increasing and decreasing.

The second row of square stitch is the hardest row in the whole piece (*as the beads are not fixed and slide around*), so bear this in mind when starting an item. It is much easier to work 50 rows x 5 beads high, than 5 rows x 50 beads high. So, as a general rule (*and all rules are made to be broken*) I thread up the lesser amount of beads when starting a piece and turn the chart sideways if necessary.

 The beaded arrow on the chart indicates the direction of the hole in the bead in relation to the chart. When working square stitch turn the chart so that the arrow is vertical (as shown on the left). When working brick stitch the arrow should be horizontal (as shown on the right).

Sizes given for the length of bracelets and straps should be adjusted to suit yourself. When making a bracelet you should also make allowance for the length the findings and closure will take up. It is not difficult to shorten or lengthen a bracelet, but it is much easier to take this into account before you start a project rather than when you finish and find you have to unpick. My first bracelet ended up as an anklet!

Now these words of warning,

"Beading is addictive!"

You will never have enough beads. You will buy impulsively a lot of beads. You will NEVER have the right colours for your current project and to top it all off, you will not want to use those special beautiful beads you couldn't live without, because then you won't have them any more!............*Jill.*

Basic Materials, Tools & Tips

THE DESIGN

By using square stitch you can have a wealth of designs at your finger tips. Using a cross stitch chart with no fractional stitches and minimal back stitch will translate very nicely into a beaded item and the majority of the designs in Jill Oxton's Cross Stitch & Beading are charts of this nature!

THE BEADS

In most cases you will get a more elegant beaded item in square stitch (brick or peyote stitch) if you use Japanese Cylinder Beads. These come in a wide variety of colours, they do not need presorting (as they are very uniform in size) and lie flat, giving an elegant, even appearance to the beading. Other beads can be used for embellishing your pieces.

THE NEEDLE

Japanese cylinder beads have thin walls and a large hole. Most of these will take a No. 28 Tapestry Needle. This needle is short, very easy to thread as it has a large eye and is blunt. The disadvantage being that the eye can break easily, so keep a plentiful supply in your workbox.

I also use beading needles when the tapestry needle doesn't fit and find the John James Size 10 Tapestry Pointed Short Beading Needle excellent, but it is harder to thread.

Avoid forcing a needle through a bead as you may break it, instead change to a finer needle or discard the bead. If the needle is tight the first time through the bead discard it as it could break when working subsequent rows.

If you have trouble threading your needles, remember that a needle's eye has a right and wrong side to it. Try rotating the needle so the reverse side of the eye is facing you and this should prove much easier.

THE THREAD

I prefer Nymo D which is a very strong, but fine, multifilament nylon thread available in a wide variety of colours. It works particularly well with a blunt beading needle.

Pre-stretch your Nymo thread by pulling it inch by inch through your fingers and stretching it at the same time. This is particularly useful for removing the curls from the thread when you are getting to

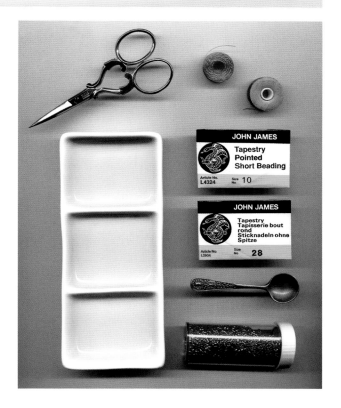

the end of a bobbin and could also help if you have a very loose tension.

I have also found that Black Nymo D tends to be thicker than some other colours. You will need to keep this in mind if you are doing a lot of weaving back and forth or if your beads have small holes.

Match your thread to the main colour of your beads and bear in mind that if you are using transparent beads, the thread will affect their colour. This can be an advantage as well as a disadvantage.

Cut your thread as long as you can manage it. You will find there is an optimum working length for you, this is when you achieve the minimum amount of twists and tangles. I cut my thread about twice the length of my outstretched arm and find this a workable length.

Do not use cotton thread for beading as it is not as strong as nylon and will rot after a period of time.

GETTING ORGANISED

Some of the most useful things I have for beading are my inexpensive ceramic sauce dishes. They have sloped sides and are heavy so are not easily dislodged. I use these to hold my beads when stitching.

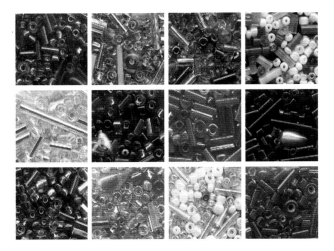

As beads bounce, I use an antique salt spoon to remove the beads from their container. You could use a plastic spoon, but I do think if you use beautiful things it makes you feel more beautiful.

To store my beads, I use clear plastic vials with screw top lids (*not pop top or your beads will go everywhere*) purchased from an outlet that distributes vials to chemists (or buy them from your local chemist). Using a permanent felt tip pen, I mark the bead colour on the side of the container and on the lid. Being clear, these vials can be placed on their side in a drawer and you can see at a glance the colours. A cheaper alternative are plastic zip lock bags.

I use an old pair of embroidery scissors as quite often they are used to cut fine-gauge wire.

A hemmed corduroy square between 20cm to 30cm (8" to 12") square is also very useful, particularly when unpicking, as the beads do not bounce on it. Some beaders I know like to place their beads on it instead of using containers such as a ceramic dish.

I take out enough beads for an hour or so as a safeguard against spilling or the cat jumping onto my workboard. For a major spill place a nylon stocking over the hose of the vacuum to collect them.

A metal board with magnetic strips such as those produced by LoRan are ideal for holding your chart. The magnetic strips are excellent to use to keep your place.

DO'S & DON'TS

If you have to unpick, unthread your needle as you can get into a real tangle if you run your needle back through the beads.

Don't change the type of thread you use within a piece as this can affect the tension and cause distortion of the beading.

Don't use super-glue on your beads, it doesn't work and can affect the finish. E6000 is a tested glue to use with beading. Imported from the USA, it is strong, clear and dries quickly. Always test your beads by placing some into a drop of glue to see if there are any adverse reactions between the bead and the glue before using any glues.

If your needle does get stuck in your beading, pull it through with a small pair of needle-nose pliers. After a little experience you can judge whether the bead will break or not. Unfortunately you will have to break a few beads to gain this experience.

If you make a mistake earlier in your beading which you haven't picked up, you can correct it by crushing the bead with pliers and adding the correct bead. This will not be perfect as thread will show. You can also use acrylic paint or a permanent marker to colour correct the bead, or you can just let it be, keeping in mind that the beauty of something handmade is in it's imperfections.

Avoid using anodised beads as the colour can wear off. You can seal them with a sealer such as Krylon (*from the USA*) but I would rather steer clear of them. Our example below shows what can happen with anodised beads after a period of wear.

THE TURTLE AMULET BAG IS FROM JILL OXTON'S CROSS STITCH, ISSUE 43.

When storing my beaded items, I place them in chocolate boxes, and use sheets of felt or tissues to protect them from rubbing against each other.

Base metal findings can be protected by painting them with clear nail polish so the plating doesn't wear off so quickly.

At the end of every project, sort out your beads and place them back into their storage containers. It is amazing how quickly they can build up and you can end up with a large number of beads that you are unable to sort.

WIRED UP

Wire can be threaded through the square stitch to give it more shape. I use 34 gauge wire and thread it though the beading when it is completed. This has been used in our examples on the right.

The Beaded Union Jack Butterfly Brooch (right) was worked in square stitch using a No. 28 Tapestry Needle, Miyuki Delica Beads, Grey Nymo D Thread and 34 gauge wire, with a two hole brooch back. I must warn you that when making this brooch I did not care what the back of the brooch looked like, I was only interested in the front (the brooch back shows wire wrapped around it, but it was tidy).

I turned the chart sideways so the hole in the bead was running horizontally on the butterfly. This made it easier to thread the wire in the correct position.

The wire branch was made by cutting a length of 34 gauge wire approximately 26cm (10') in length, folding it about ten times and then twisting it and folding it back onto itself until it was the desired size and a pleasing shape. This was then secured to the brooch back finding by wrapping wire tightly around both the branch and the brooch back.

The cocoon was made by working an irregular shaped spiral rope chain using Delica beads and Nymo thread and was secured to the brooch back by wrapping a length of wire around the cocoon, brooch and branch.

The antennae and legs were made using 34 gauge wire. I cut four pieces of 34 gauge wire into 30cm (12") lengths for the legs. From the outside edge I pushed the wire through the row of beads where the leg was to be positioned and then turned and came back down the next row, ending with the wire coming out of the same bead. This step was repeated for the other three legs. Each pair of wires

was twisted and the legs bent into shape. The excess wire was then wrapped around the cocoon and brooch back to attach the butterfly.

The antennae were made using 34 gauge wire (only one thickness this time). The wire was curved by holding the beadwork firmly where the wire was positioned with my left hand. With my right hand, I held the wire tightly between thumb and forefinger and pulled my fingers down the length of the wire as if I was stretching it. This movement also helped to unkink and straighten the wire when threading it through the beads.

Although this method is fiddly and time consuming, I felt it was well worth the effort.

The Butterflies are from Jill Oxton's Cross Stitch & Beading, Issue 46.

The Fuchsias are from Jill Oxton's Cross Stitch & Beading, Issue 48.

MIYUKI DELICA BEADS

are a Japanese cylinder bead and come in two sizes, DBR (medium) 11/0 and DBL (large) 8/0. They are very uniform in size and need minimum grading. Cylindrical in shape with thin walls and large holes, they allow many thread passings and create a uniform smooth surface, similar in a lot of ways to Oreton mesh.

The majority of our beading uses Delica size 11/0.

Delica's are not precisely square and we find that when working square stitch with Delica 11/0's you get approximately 7 beads per centimetre x 6 rows per centimetre. Therefore if I wanted to work a square shape 1cm x 1cm as accurately as possible I would thread up 7 beads and work 6 rows.

Left: pictured at approximate actual size, the daffodil and vase have been worked in Delica 11/0 and the daffodil below has been worked in Delica DBL 8/0.

IN A 3GMS PACKET you will get approximately

500 x Delica 11/0 *or*
90 x Delica 8/0.

Delica cylinder beads are also available in a hex cut (DBC), having five sides. They are in the same sizes as mentioned above and I occasionally use them if I need a particular colour, or for fringing.

JAPANESE SEED BEADS

come in two sizes 11/0 and 15/0. We have used these on the beaded fish and the brick stitch bracelet.

Japanese Seed Beads are more uniform in size and shape than Czech and therefore need less grading. Square stitching with Japanese seed beads give you a slightly bumpy surface.

PER GRAM

You will get approximately

100 x 11/0 Japanese Seed Beads
250 x 15/0 Japanese Seed Beads

Pictured above: The pink fish has moderate use of size 11/0 Japanese seed beads in the body. The beads around the eyes and gills of the fish are size 15/0 Japanese seed beads.

Above: Using the same increases and decreases as for the pink fish, we alternated size 11/0 Delica and Japanese Seed Beads in the body. This caused the body to be baggier and so we "sculpted" the top to give back more shape (see page 64).

CZECH SEED BEADS

come in a multitude of sizes and are sold in bags or on hanks. They are not round but have a donut like appearance and are irregularly shaped, needing grading for square stitch and other precise stitches.

Czech Seed Beads are ideal for use in fringes and other embellishments.

We used these for our fringes on the amulet bags, the centre of flowers and the eyes for the fish.

OTHER TYPES OF BEADS

BUGLE BEADS are lengths of cut glass cane, coming in many sizes, colours and finishes.

CHARLOTTES are Czech Seed Beads with one or two facets ground onto their surface.

FACETED BEADS are hand or machine cut to produce multiple flat surfaces which reflect the light.

GEMSTONE CHIPS are polished chips of semi precious stone.

SOME BEAD FINISHES

ALABASTER: Milky finish.

CEYLON OR LUSTER: Shiny pearly type finishes.

DYED: *Dyes can wear off or fade.*

IRIS: Multicoloured shiny finish.

MATT: Flat or dull finish.

METALLIC/GALVANISED: Metallic finish. *This can wear off.*

SATIN: Frosted finish *due to many tiny air bubbles pulled through the forming molten glass.*

SILVERLINED: Mirror like lining in the hole in the bead.

TRANSPARENT: See through. *The thread can greatly affect the* colour of the bead.

Turquoise & Gold

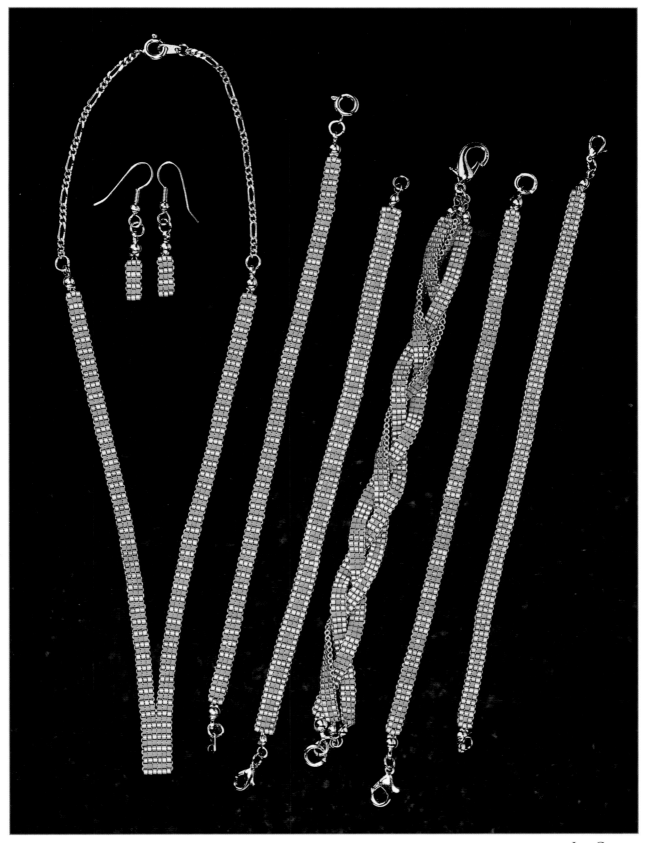

BY JILL OXTON

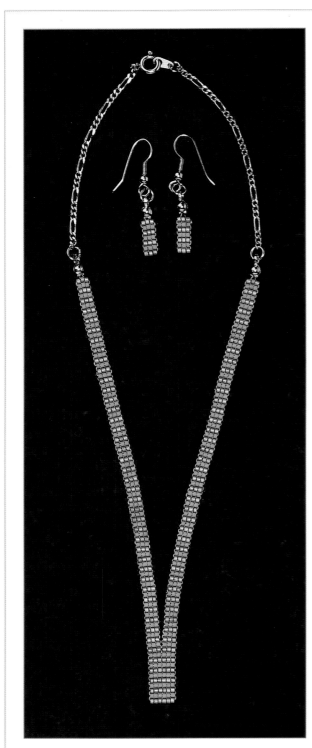

Turquoise
Necklace & Earrings

The join in the necklace should lie just below the throat to sit properly.

We used a gold Figaro chain, cut it off 6.5cm (2 ⁵/₈") either side of the clasp and attached a 5mm slip ring to each end. Cover tips were attached to either end of the beaded necklace, which were then joined to the slip rings on the chain.

Any of the bracelet designs can be used to make this necklace.

Start beading at the bottom of the necklace by threading up six gold beads.

The arrow indicates the direction of threading up the beads.

Using square stitch method 7c throughout, work ten rows x six beads wide and then work one split section of the necklace three beads wide.

The split section of the necklace is 13cm (5 ¹/₈") long.

Join in a new length of thread and work the other side three beads wide, matching up the design.

The Earrings

Work the earrings by threading up three gold beads and working seven rows of the chart. Cover tips and slip rings attach the beading to the shepherd's hooks.

See page 76 for attaching findings.

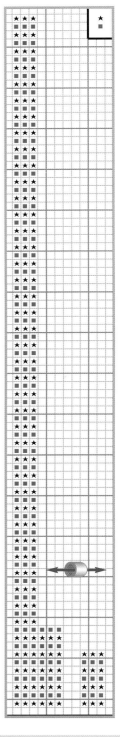

Start the second half of the split section of the necklace on the same side as you did for the first side, or else you will have a reflection line in your beading as the beads are angled differently. This will be more noticeable with shiny beads.

The easiest way is to make sure your beading is turned in the same position as the chart, before commencing the second side.

Discount jewellery stores are a good source of chain. Expecially the sale items. These come in a wide variety of styles, weights and lengths. Purchase the chain and remove the attachments, they may be useful sometime in the future.

9k gold findings can be purchased from manufacturing jewellers for those extra special pieces or use discarded and broken jewellery.

Turquoise Bracelets

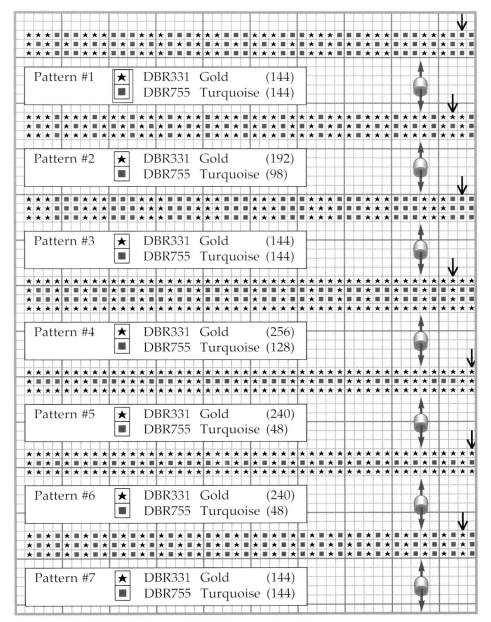

| Pattern #1 | ★ | DBR331 Gold | (144) |
| | ■ | DBR755 Turquoise | (144) |

| Pattern #2 | ★ | DBR331 Gold | (192) |
| | ■ | DBR755 Turquoise | (98) |

| Pattern #3 | ★ | DBR331 Gold | (144) |
| | ■ | DBR755 Turquoise | (144) |

| Pattern #4 | ★ | DBR331 Gold | (256) |
| | ■ | DBR755 Turquoise | (128) |

| Pattern #5 | ★ | DBR331 Gold | (240) |
| | ■ | DBR755 Turquoise | (48) |

| Pattern #6 | ★ | DBR331 Gold | (240) |
| | ■ | DBR755 Turquoise | (48) |

| Pattern #7 | ★ | DBR331 Gold | (144) |
| | ■ | DBR755 Turquoise | (144) |

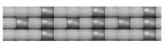

The arrow indicates the centre of chart. Turn chart 90° to work other half.

It is easier to thread up three (or four) beads and work approximately 97 rows.

A bracelet is about 19cm (7 ¹/₂") from end to end, including findings.

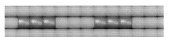

Aim for a beaded length of around 16cm (6 ¹/₄").

Delica Beads are commonly sold in 3 gram packets, giving you 500 beads per packet.

You get approximately 180 beads per gram with Delica's.

The number in brackets ( ) in the colour key indicates the number of beads required for a 16cm (6 ¹/₄") length of beading.

SEE PAGE 70 FOR SQUARE STITCH INSTRUCTIONS AND PAGE 76 FOR ATTACHING FINDINGS.

The bracelet pictured on page 9 was plaited for photographic purposes. To bead a plaited bracelet; following the pattern, work 5 rows by 9 beads high, then divide this and work three lengths by 3 beads high and plait. Ending with 5 rows of 9 beads.

We used square stitch with Delica Round (DBR) Matt Beads, Copper Nymo D Thread and a No. 28 Tapestry Needle

★ DBR331 Gold
■ DBR755 Turquoise

FINDINGS

You will also need the following for each bracelet:

2 x 5mm Jump Rings

2 x Bead Tips/Cover Tips

1 x Bracelet Clasp & Ring

BY GWENDOLYN OXTON

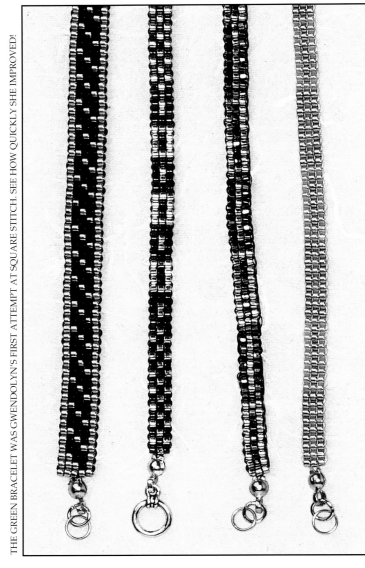

THE GREEN BRACELET WAS GWENDOLYN'S FIRST ATTEMPT AT SQUARE STITCH. SEE HOW QUICKLY SHE IMPROVED!

Gwendolyn used square stitch, method 7c (see page 71) with Miyuki Delica Round (DBR) Beads, Nymo D thread and a No. 28 Tapestry Needle.

Bracelets 1, 2 and 3 used Black Nymo D, Bracelet 3 (Blue) used Silver Nymo D.

You will also need the following findings for each bracelet:

2 x 5mm Jump Rings
2 x Bead Tips/Cover Tips
1 x Bracelet Clasp & Ring

Bracelet #1

★	DBR34 Gold	(301)
🔲	DBR10 Black	(194)

Bracelet #2

★	DBR 32 White Gold	(139)
🔲	DBR105 Dark Red	(158)

Bracelet #3

★	DBR34 Gold	(155)
🔲	DBR27 Dark Green	(142)

Bracelet #3

★	DBR 34 Gold	(155)
🔲	DBR257 Light Blue	(142)

Turban Brooches by Di Noyce

*S*imple to make and no two the same, these delightful Turban Brooches are made by beading a rectangle in square stitch, fringing one short edge and then attaching it to a porcelain face using Kikusui double-sided tape or glue.

The hat is folded and twisted around the top of the head and fringes are added to the sides.

Use them framed, as brooches, set on to a necklace, or to decorate bags.

Handpainted porcelain faces were obtained from:

Little People in Porcelain,
PO Box 49
Everton Park
Queensland Australia 4053

Ph +61 (07) 3356 7172.

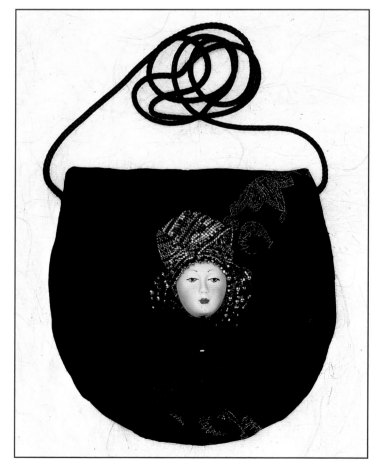

Turban Brooch

BY DI NOYCE

Stitch Count 30 high x 39 rows

STITCHES USED:
SQUARE STITCH (see page 70)
FRINGING (see page 72)

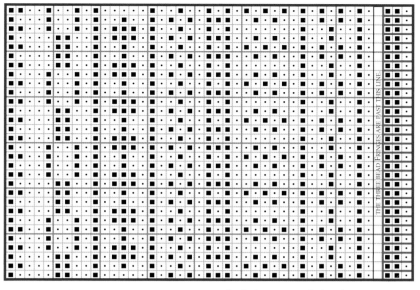

The three bead fringes are past this line.

Red Turban
•	DBR 105	Red	(699)
■	DBC 34	Gold	(561)

Green Turban
•	DBR 373	Green	(699)
■	DBC 34	Gold	(561)

Blue & White Gold Turban *(in frame)*
•	DBR 35	White Gold	(699)
■	DBR 86	Blue	(561)

Black & Purple Turban
•	DBR 10	Black	(699)
■	DBR 29	Bronze Iris	(561)

Citrine Turban
•	DBR 35	White Gold	(699)
■	DBC 121	Topaz	(561)

Black & Gold Turbans *(Bag & Necklace)*
•	DBR 34	Gold	(699)
■	DBR 10	Black	(561)

Dull Black Turban
•	DBR 380	Green/Pink	(699)
■	DBR 10	Black	(561)

MATERIALS

1 x Brooch Face *(see page 13)*
5 gms Japanese Cylinder Beads in two contrasting colours
Accent Beads for Fringe
Nymo D Thread
No. 28 Tapestry Needle
Kikusui Double-sided Tape
Brooch Bar 15mm wide
Card or Perforated Plastic

METHOD: Work above chart using square stitch. Arrow shows the direction of hole in the bead in relation to the chart. This will need to be soft and drapey so use method 7a or 7b (see page 71).

When complete and using the darkest colour, work a three bead fringe on one end of the beading.

Using double-sided tape, attach the beading to the forehead of the porcelain face, curving it slightly around the face.

Twist and fold the top section of beading until happy with the effect. Stitch down with matching thread.

Add long fringes of varying lengths to each side, eg: three fringes on left hand side and five fringes on right hand side.

Cover card or canvas with felt or fabric. Stitch and glue the brooch bar to the back.

Attach this to the back of the head. You will find two small holes, (on the top and bottom of the porcelain head) to use.

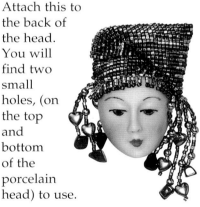

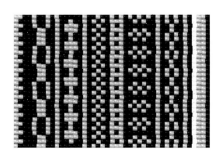

Pictured left is the pattern using the colours indicated on the chart. Pictured right, the colour value of the beads has been swapped. So, besides the variation you get using different colours, you can also achieve a different look by swapping the bead colours around.

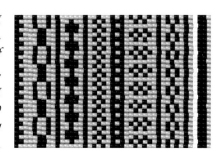

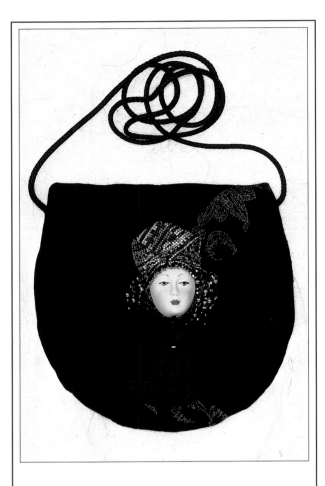

To Make Up Bag

The evening bag was made up from a kit supplied by

Sanshi,
115 Palmerston Street,
Mosman Park, Western Australia 6012
Ph/Fax (08)9384 8244
www.sanshi.com.au

MATERIALS

Silk Tassel 5cms (2") long
Sanshi Silk Evening Bag Kit
Turban Brooch *(see page 13)*

METHOD

Make up the brooch as detailed on page 15, using beads in colours to match the bag fabric. Attach the tassel through the hole under the chin of the porcelain face.

Make up the evening bag following the instructions supplied with kit.

Pin the brooch to the front of the bag.

To Make Up Necklace

MATERIALS

Silk Tassel 5cms (2") long
Assorted beads
Necklace Findings
Nymo D *(use two strands for stringing beads)*
Turban Brooch *(see page 13)*

METHOD

Make up the brooch as detailed on page 15, using beads in colours to compliment the necklace. Attach the tassel through the hole under the chin of the porcelain face.

Using beads of various shapes and sizes, string up twelve strands of desired length and make up into a necklace.

Flatten out necklace in centre and attach brooch, then twist the necklace on both sides to make the strands sit together.

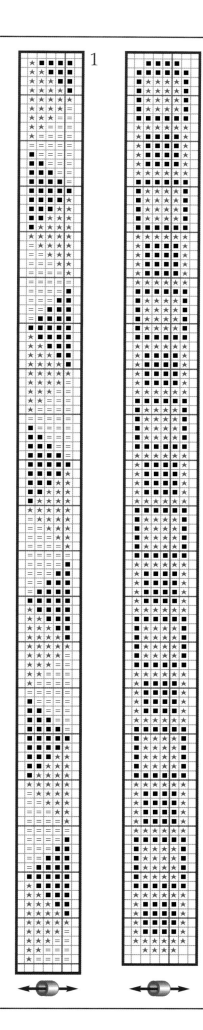

Metallic Bracelets

BY ERIKA BANNA

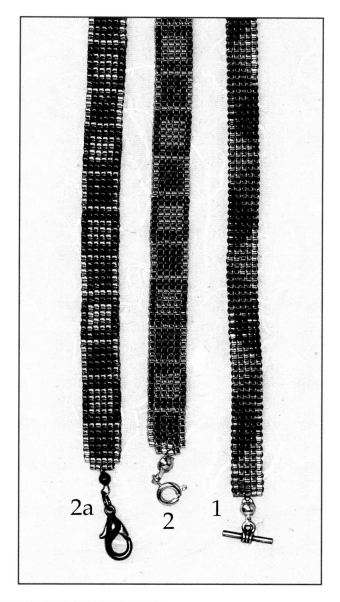

> *There are approximately 500 beads in a 3gm packet of Delica's.*

Erika used square stitch (method 7c) with Miyuki Delica Round (DBR) Beads 11/0, Copper Nymo D Thread and a No. 28 Tapestry Needle.

You will also need the following findings for each bracelet:

2 x 5mm Jump Rings
2 x Bead Tips/Cover Tips
1 x Bracelet Clasp & Ring

Triangle Bracelet #1

★	DBR31	Gold	(175)
=	DBR144	Brown	(160)
■	DBR23	L.Bronze Iris	(160)

Square Bracelet #2

★	DBR 34	Gold	(292)
■	DBR29	M.Bronze Iris	(292)

Square Bracelet #2a

★	DBR 34	Gold	(292)
■	DBR23	L.Bronze Iris	(292)

Zig Zag Choker

BY GWENDOLYN OXTON

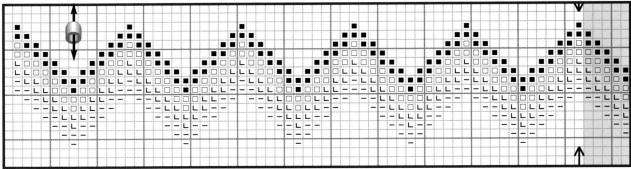

This simple but effective design is the perfect opportunity for you to practice your increasing and decreasing in square stitch.

We used the Zig Zag design as a choker, but it would also make a lovely bracelet and would be most elegant as a trim for the cuffs and edges of a simple light weight black or navy jacket.

DBR		COLOUR	QTY
10	■	Black	270
25	□	Metallic Blue Iris	270
6	L	Gunmetal AB	270
510	–	Met.Blue/Purple Iris	270

YOU WILL ALSO NEED:

2 x Silver Covertips

4 x Silver 3mm Jump rings

1 x Silver Necklace Closure Findings

1 x Silver Chain

Needlenose Pliers to attach findings

Clear Nail Polish or Glue

Gwendolyn used square stitch (see page 70) with Miyuki Delica 11/0 Japanese Cylinder Beads, a No. 28 Tapestry Needle and one strand of Black Nymo D thread.

STITCHES USED:

SQUARE STITCH

plus Increasing & Decreasing

(see pages 70 & 74)

The blue beaded arrow on the chart indicates the direction of the hole in the beads. The black arrows indicate the centre point of the choker.

The chart above only shows half of the design we worked for the model. Repeat the pattern until there are 10 points at the bottom, or until it is the desired length.

Attach enough chain so the choker fits snugly around neck.

Little Boxes

STITCHES USED:

SQUARE STITCH

BRICK STITCH

FRINGING

Bracelet patterns can also be used on the sides of boxes. For the most effective use, place them on the sides of the lid. Dress up a plain box by adding charms as we did for the chest, or embellishing the lid with flowers.

To Make a Box

BOX SIDES: Work the side strip in **square stitch** using method 7c or 7d as it should be rigid (*see page 70*). Thread up the beads in the direction indicated by the beaded arrow. Join the ends of the strip together using square stitch. You will find it easier if you use a different coloured bead on the corner edges to indicate your fold lines as we did for the square box, pictured on the right.

BOX BASE: The four bottom sections are sewn separately in square stitch and then joined to the box sides with a loose tension as you need these sections to fold over at a right angle. (*See page 22 for joining the top of the box*).

Join the triangles together using square stitch and then work the ⓑ symbol shown on the chart using **brick stitch** (*see page 66*).

To make the box more rigid, line the sides and base with card (*see page 21*) and cover the card with fabric, wrapping paper or paint with acrylic paint.

Variations on a Box

CHRISTMAS ORNAMENT: Work a cube and hang a tassel or fringes from it. To make a cube work two bases, one on the top and the other on the bottom.

CHEST: Work two complete bases, the lid being shorter in height. Line the box with fabric covered card and attach a padlock charm to the front. You could also make a hinge out of beads for the back.

SQUARE BOX: Work a base and a lid. Each of the four side sections of the lid is two beads wider to enable it to fit over the base (*see picture on right*).

RECTANGULAR BOX: Increase the number of columns worked in the second and fourth sections of the chart, for both the lid and the base.

Work the sides of the lid wider than the base so the lid will fit over the base.

To get a nice corner edge on the sides of a box fold the corners on a bead, not between beads.

The base and top of the lid are worked in four individual sections and then joined together. To avoid puckering and to ensure the flattest surface, make a temporary form/lining out of cardboard to keep the box in the right shape before joining the base sections together. When joining the lid sections together, place the lid on top of the box and then join together.

Bottom right shows the box with its permanent lining in it.This helps the box keep it's shape.

These boxes took about twelve hours each to make, so I suggest you work a small one first, to get an understanding of how they are constructed and how the beads fit together on the base and lid when joining them.

Don't worry if they are a little floppy as a lining works wonders! But, be careful of thread buildup as there are a lot of ends that need to be woven into the beading.

Be kind to yourself on your learning projects, embellishments can hide a lot of mistakes and we all learn from our mistakes.

<u>BLACK NYMO D thread is thicker</u> than most of the other Nymo D colours I have used. Therefore take extra care of thread build up when you use it making boxes, as are there are a lot of ends to weave in.

Lining a box helps it to keep its shape, particularly if the stitch used is not a rigid one, such as square stitch.

The larger the box, the more support it needs.

The thickness of card depends on the size of the box. Use a thin but stiff card for small boxes, but the larger the box, the thicker the card used to line it.

Card has a grain. If you roll it with the grain it will crease smoothly, if you roll it against the grain it will 'crack' and will crease roughly.

Scoring a card before folding it, gives a cleaner fold. To score card, use the back/blunt edge of a knife.

Padding the base and the top of the lid (not the sides), of a small box with a satin type fabric can make a box look more luxurious and finished off.

If you do not want to make a different sized lid, you can make the top and bottom the same diameter, but make the lid about one third of the height and use your lining to hold the lid in place.

Lining Square Boxes

Ways to cut a box from card. Our diagrams show two ways for cutting and scoring card to make a box shape. Use matching card, or cover with fabric, clipping and overlapping fabric at the edges of the card. Glue or doublesided tape can be used to stick the fabric to the card.

Lining Round Boxes

It is much easier to line a round box, all that is needed is a strip of card to fit inside the box, with a little overlap to join the ends together. The base is circular and should slide in after the sides have been lined.

If you do not want to make a different sized lid, you can make the top and bottom the same diameter, but make the lid about a third of the height and use your lining to hold the lid in place. To do this you will need two linings on the base of the box. The first, the same height as the round box, the second inner most lining, taller than the box. This must also be tall enough to hold the lid in place. The lid of the box only needs one lining, but this must be able to slip over the innermost lining of the base. Once again, padding the lid and base can give a more luxurious finish to the box.

1. Lining A Small Square Box.

Place double-sided tape on all four corners, to hold the lining together.

Fold cut corners over to the back of lining and stick down.

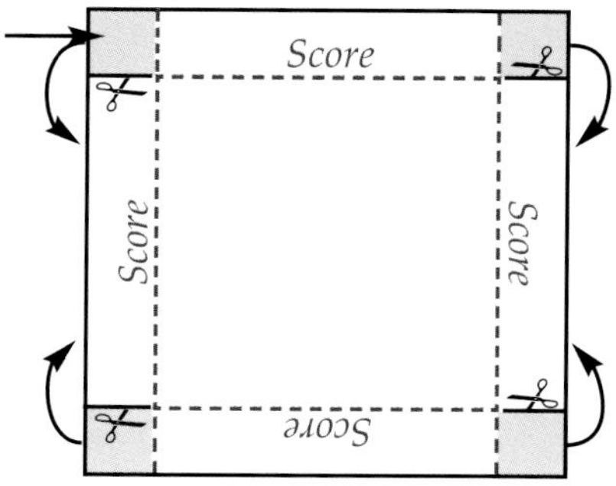

(Diagram: Square with "Score" labels on each side, scissors at corners)

2. Lining A Small Square Box

Overlap	Score	Score	Score	Score	Side Sections (4)

Base

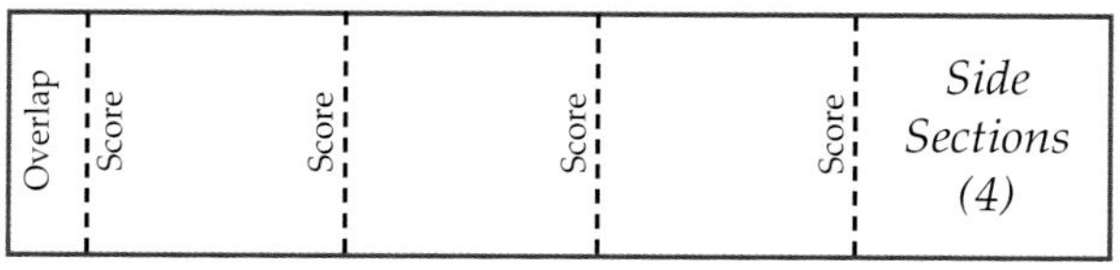

Cut the base slightly smaller than the sides (so it fits inside the lining card) and place it inside the box.

Lining A Round Box

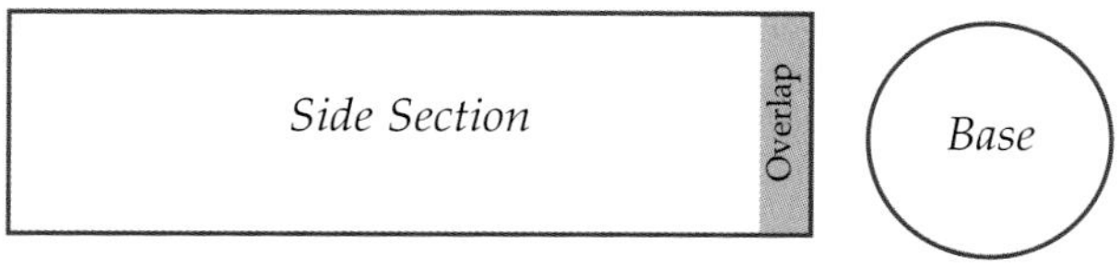

Side Section	Overlap	Base

The Diagram on the right shows the lining for a round box with a lid made the same size as the base. Make a double lining, the outer lining (red, next to the beading) should be slightly lower than the beading. The inner lining (brown) should be higher than the box, but not as high as the lid, as the lid edge should rest on the upper edge of the base.

Remember the rule, measure twice and cut once. Check each cut and score against your beading and place the complete lining inside the box to check it fits before finally sticking the sides together.

Also refer to the notes on page 23 for the Banded Rectangular Chest, pictured on pages 19 and 20.

The Square Box *(also see page 20).*

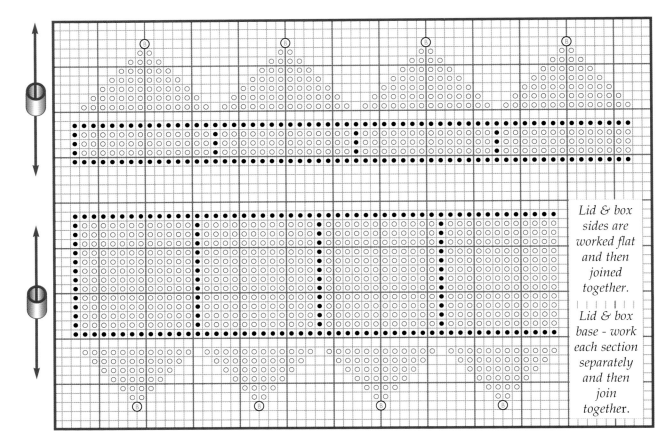

Lid & box sides are worked flat and then joined together.

|‖‖‖‖‖|

Lid & box base - work each section separately and then join together.

Joining the top and base of the box

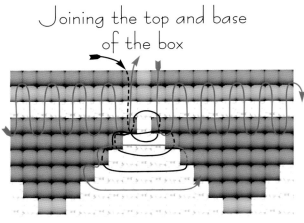

The diagram on the left shows the thread path for joining triangles and closing the base and top. When closing these, pull the beads together, but not so tightly that they buckle. The last four beads to close up the centre of the lid and base are worked using brick stitch.

We used square stitch with Matte Metallic Miyuki Delica Beads 11/0, Grey Nymo D Thread and a No. 28 Tapestry Needle.

DBR380 Green Pink as the main colour.

DBR331 Yellow Gold as the trim colour.

○	DBR380 (7gms) *1136 beads*
●	DBR331 (2gms) *303 beads*
B	DBR331 Brick Stitch *(8)*

Where increasing by two beads is too much and by one bead is too little, after the lid was worked I tightened the corners by first squeezing each corner flat and then tying a length of thread through the main colour bead on each side of the corner bead. This was then knotted tightly and the ends woven into the beading, ensuring the lid was a good fit.

Banded Rectangular Chest *(also see page 20).*

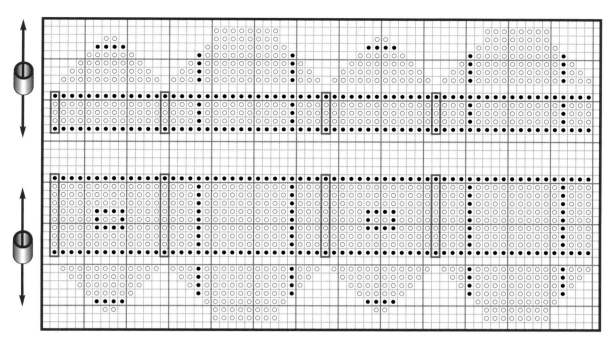

Because the lid was the same size as the base, we added an extra inner lining in the base to enable the lid to stay on. (See page 21). This lining was a strip of card, higher than the beaded base (and scored and folded in the appropriate places) which the lid would slip onto. This was stuck onto the outer lining using Kikusui double-sided tape. It is best to use thin card for the lid and thicker card for both base linings, to ensure that the lid will fit over the inner lining.

A padlock charm was stitched to the box to finish it off.

We used Matte Metallic Miyuki Delica Beads 11/0 with Black Nymo D Thread and a No. 28 Tapestry Needle. Square stitch was used throughout.

- ● DBR331 (2gms) *368 beads*
- ○ DBR324 (7gms) *1104 beads*

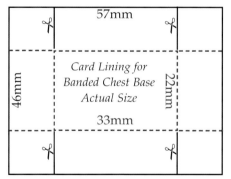

Card Lining for Banded Chest Base Actual Size

57mm · 46mm · 22mm · 33mm

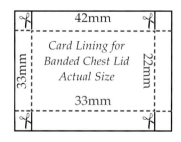

Card Lining for Banded Chest Lid Actual Size

42mm · 33mm · 22mm · 33mm

I made a bit of a mess of the lining, but managed to save it. The gold card that I used was too thin and not rigid enough!

To rectify this another strip of card was added to both the inner and outer linings, sticking them together with Kikusui double-sided tape. There were now a lot of raw edges to be touched up, so the entire lining was re-painted with gold acrylic paint.

It is advisable to place the lining inside the box to check it is the right size and that the lid sits correctly before securing.

To secure the lining to the lid, double-sided tape was used all over the outside of the lid lining as the sides were so short.

Only one piece of double-sided tape was used on the bottom of the base lining to secure it to the beading as it was a tight fit.

Jack In The Box

Colour Key for The Box

Miyuki Delica (DBR) 11/0
Bead Colour Key QTY

+	DBR721	Yellow		1004
●	DBR723	Red		381
B	DBR726	Blue		376
✕	DBR656	Green		285

Jack's colour key is on page 25.

The box was worked using silver Nymo D Thread and a No. 28 Tapestry Needle.

Other Materials Required:

Nymo D Thread -
silver or light grey
Thick Card
Cotton Wool
Yellow Acrylic Paint
Double-sided Tape or Glue
26 Gauge Wire
2 Drinking Straws *4mm
diameter (ours were from
Kentucky Chicken).*

Construction Details

1. Lid and Sides are worked in square stitch (method 7C as you want it to be rigid, *see page 71*) using Nymo D in silver. Start from the left hand side of the chart and when finished, square stitch B to C.

2. Box Base: The four bottom sections are sewn separately in square stitch and then joined to the box sides (with a loose tension as you need these sections to fold over at a right angle). *See page 22 for instructions on joining these sections.*

3. Join the sides of the triangles together and then, using the same piece of thread, work two **brick stitch** on each edge to form a circle and then one brick stitch on each edge to close up the centre of the base.

Brick stitch is the symbol within a circle on the chart.

(continued on page 25)

Stitches Used
Square Stitch (see page 70)
Brick Stitch (see page 66)
Fringing (see page 72)

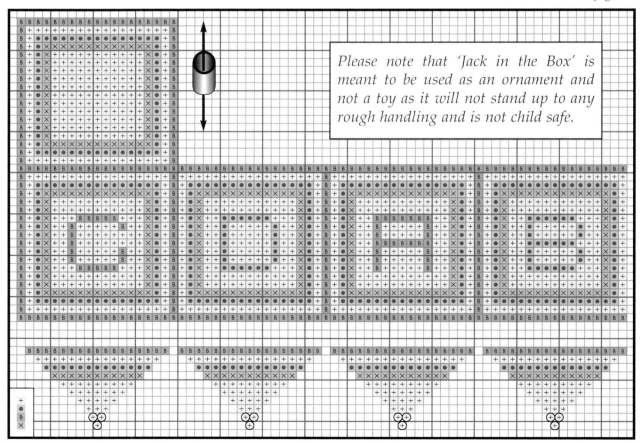

Please note that 'Jack in the Box' is meant to be used as an ornament and not a toy as it will not stand up to any rough handling and is not child safe.

Jack Brick Stitch Chart

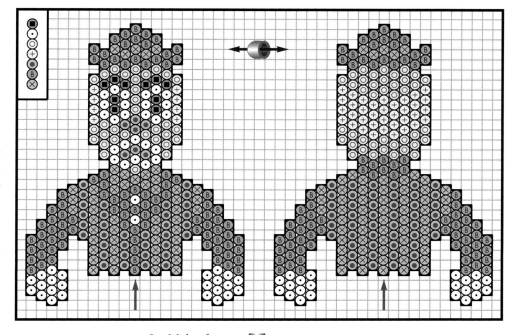

The beaded arrow indicates the direction of the hole in the beads.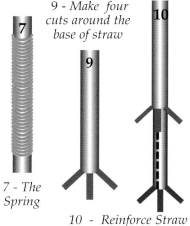

The red arrows indicate the starting point. →

Construction Details
continued from page 24

4. Brick stitch Jack and stuff the head with a small pinch of cotton wool when sewing up the sides.

5. Make a card lining for the box, consisting of four sides and a base.

6. Make two more bases out of card to fit inside the cardboard lining. Punch a hole in the centre of these, large enough for the straw to fit through and stick together. Place double-sided tape on the bottom.

7. The Spring: Wrap 26 gauge wire around one straw until it measures about 3.5cm (1³/₈") compressed or 6cm (2³/₈") sprung. Wrap the wire as tightly as you can without buckling the straw and then twist one end of the wrapped wire, while holding the other end, to tighten the spring.

8. Push the spring on the straw into Jack's body as far as it goes and then screw it in a little further.

9. Remove the straw from the spring and cut to 5cm (2") in length. *Make four cuts evenly around one end of the straw 1cm (¹/₂") long and bend and fan the ends out to form a base.*

7 - The Spring

9 - Make four cuts around the base of straw

10 - Reinforce Straw

10. Reinforce the straw by cutting another 5cm of straw and repeating * to *. Cut this straw all the way along the length and fit inside the first straw gently bending and fanning out the base.

11. Place the straw through the hole in the card base, place doublesided tape on the base of the straw and stick to the card lining.

12. Paint the lining and straw using the yellow acrylic paint and let dry.

13. Gently place Jack and the spring onto the straw.

14. By positioning the spring so the edge is just a little above the straw, Jack will move if you gently shake or tap the box.

Colour Key for Jack

MIYUKI DELICA ROUND 11/0

	BEAD COLOUR KEY		QTY
■	DBR10	Black	10
•	DBR351	White	75
○	DBR205	Flesh	74
+	DBR721	Yellow	45
●	DBR723	Red	90
B	DBR726	Blue	174
✕	DBR656	Green	116

JACK was worked in brick stitch using silver Nymo D Thread and a No. 28 Tapestry Needle.

1. Work one front and one back. Join together by placing on top of each other and sew through the side beads.

2. Join one side and top of head and then place a tiny pinch of cotton wool inside the head to pad it out. Don't use too much or you will have a gap between the pieces. Use a toothpick to push the stuffing into the correct position.

3. Work three and four bead fringes (1 bead picot) around the sides and bottom of the yellow section of head for the hair.

4. Jack is now ready to mount onto the spring, see pages 24 and 25 for construction details for assembling *Jack in the Box*.

Large Round Pot (also see notes on page 28)

The large pot was worked using Japanese Cylinder Beads, Nymo D Thread and a No. 28 Tapestry Needle. The sides were worked as charted using square stitch and the base and top were worked using tubular concentric brick stitch, see pattern instructions below. The base was lined to keep it rigid.

STITCHES USED
SQUARE STITCH (SEE PAGE 70)
TUBULAR CONCENTRIC BRICK STITCH (SEE PAGE 67)

Miyuki Delica 11/0			QTY
=	DBR27	D. Green	1914
●	DBR627	L. Green	567
□	DBR694	Purple	75
▽	DBR625	Pink	100

Chart left is for the side of the base.

Chart below is for the side of the lid.

This pot involves decreasing in brick stitch. Decreasing, under previous decreases will create a nicer pattern.

BASE SIDE: 64 wide x 14 high

Using square stitch (*method 7c so that it is rigid*), work the top chart and join the short edges together to make a round. Do not cut thread.

BASE BOTTOM - Brick stitch Dark Green except for Round 2.

Round 1: (64 beads) - Using same thread, come out of the centre of one square stitched bead and brick stitch around one side edge. *Work loosely so that the beads can be pushed over at a right angle.*

Round 2: (56 L. Green beads) - *work seven, skip one*, repeat to end of round.

Round 3 Dark Green: (48 beads) - *work six, miss one*, repeat to end of round.

Round 4: (48 beads).

Round 5: (40 beads) - *work five, miss one*, repeat to end of round.

Round 6: (40 beads).

Round 7: (32 beads) - *work four, miss one*, repeat to end of round.

Round 8: (24 beads) - *work three, miss one*, repeat to end of round.

Round 9: (24 beads).

Round 10: (16 beads) - *work two, miss one*, repeat to end of round.

Round 11: (8 beads) - Starting with two beads, but missing the first space, *work one, miss one*, repeat to end.

Round 12: (4 beads) - Starting with two beads, but missing the first space, *work one, miss one*, repeat to end of round and finish off by weaving in thread ends.

LID SIDE: 72 wide x 10 high

Using square stitch (*method 7c*), work the bottom chart and join the short edges together to make a round. Do not cut thread.

LID TOP - Brick stitch Dark Green except for Round 2.

Round 1: (72 beads) - using the same thread, come out of the centre of one square stitched bead and brick stitch around one side edge. *Work loosely so that the beads can be pushed toward the centre.*

Round 2: (64 L. Green beads)- *work eight, miss one*, repeat to end of round.

Round 3: (56 beads) - *work seven, miss one*, repeat to end of round.

Round 4: (56 beads).

Round 5: (48 beads) - *work six, miss one*, repeat to end of round.

Round 6: (48 beads).

Round 7: (40 beads) - *work five, miss one*, repeat to end of round.

Round 8: (40 beads).

Round 9: (32 beads) - *work four, miss one*, repeat to end of round.

Round 10: (32 beads).

Round 11: (24 beads) - *work three, miss one*, repeat to end.

Round 12: (24 beads).

Round 13: (16 beads) - *work two, miss one*, repeat to end of round.

Round 14: (8 beads) - Starting with two beads, but missing the first space, *work one, miss one*, repeat to end of round.

Round 15: (8 beads).

Round 16: (4 beads) - Starting with two beads, but missing the first space, *work one, miss one*, repeat to end of round and finish off by weaving in thread ends.

Forget-me-not Domed Pot

STITCHES USED

SQUARE STITCH (SEE PAGE 70)
TUBULAR CONCENTRIC BRICK STITCH (SEE NOTES ON PAGE 28 AND 67)
FORGET-ME-NOTS (SEE PAGE 54)

Colour Key for Domed Pot

MIYUKI DELICA ROUND (DBR) 11/0

	BEAD	COLOUR KEY		QTY
☒	DBR10	Black	■	1451
★	DBR34	Gold	▨	13
	DBR167	Blue	▨	120
	DBR721	Yellow	□	3

Plus three small Czech glass leaves

Size of Forget-me-not Pot is approximately 3cm wide x 3cm high (1 ¼" x 1 ¼")

This Domed Pot was worked using Japanese Cylinder Beads, Nymo D Thread and a No. 28 Tapestry Needle.

The sides were worked as charted using square stitch. The base and top were worked using Tubular Concentric Brick Stitch, working from the outside into the centre, pattern details below.

Three brick stitch Forget-me-nots (page 55) were then attached to the top of the lid along with three Czech glass leaves.

The base of the box was lined to make it more rigid, see page 21.

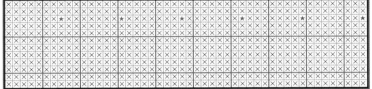

The chart above is for the side of the base.

The chart below is for the side of the lid.

> *T*REAT THE OUTSIDE EDGE OF THE JOINED SQUARE STITCH STRIP AS YOU WOULD LADDER STITCH WHEN WORKING THE FIRST ROUND OF TUBULAR CONCENTRIC BRICK STITCH FOR THE POTS.

This box involves decreasing in brick stitch. Decreasing, under previous decreases will create a nicer pattern.

Always start a brick stitch row with two beads (this is also counted as two beads).

BASE SIDE: 48 wide x 12 high

Using square stitch *(method 7c so that it is rigid)*, work the top chart and join the short edges together to make a round. Do not cut the thread.

BASE BOTTOM: This is worked using brick stitch from the bottom edge of the square stitch round.

Round 1: (40 beads) - Coming out of the centre of a square stitched bead, *Work five, miss one*, repeat to end of round.

Round 2: (40 beads) - Work brick stitch to end of round.

Round 3: (32 beads) - *Work four, miss one*, repeat to end of round.

Round 4: (24 beads) - *Work three, miss one*, repeat to end of round.

Round 5: (24 beads) - Work brick stitch to end of round.

Round 6: (16 beads) - *Work two, miss one*, repeat to end of round.

Round 7: (16 beads) - Work brick stitch to end of round.

Round 8: (8 beads) - *Work one, miss one*, repeat to end of round.

Round 9: (4) beads - *Work one, miss one*, four times. Weave in thread ends to finish off.

LID SIDE: 56 wide x 7 high

Using square stitch *(method 7c so that it is rigid)*, work the bottom chart and join the short edges together to make a round. Do not cut thread.

LID TOP: This is worked using brick stitch from the edge of the square stitch round.

Round 1: (48 beads) - Coming out of the centre of a square stitched bead, *Work six, miss one*, repeat to end of round.

Round 2: (48 beads) - Work brick stitch to end of round.

Round 3: (40 beads) - *Work five, miss one*, repeat to end of round.

Round 4: (40 beads) - Work brick stitch to end of round.

Round 5: (32 beads) - *Work four, miss one*, repeat to end of round.

Round 6: (32 beads) - Work brick stitch to end of round.

Round 7: (24 beads) - *Work three, miss one*, repeat to end of round.

Round 8: (24 beads) - Work brick stitch to end of round.

Round 9: (16 beads) - *Work two, miss one*, repeat to end of round.

Round 10: (16 beads) - Work brick stitch to end of round.

Round 11: (8 beads) - *Work one, miss one*, repeat to end of round.

Round 12: (4) beads - *Work one, miss one*, four times. Weave in thread ends to finish off.

Small Round Pot

The Small Round Pot was worked using Japanese Cylinder Beads, Nymo D Thread and a No. #28 Tapestry Needle.

The sides were worked as charted using square stitch and the base and top were worked using brick stitch, pattern details below.

The size of the Small Round Pot is approximately 2.5cm wide x 2cm high (1" wide x ³/₄" high)

STITCHES USED

SQUARE STITCH (SEE PAGE 70)
TUBULAR CONCENTRIC BRICK STITCH (SEE PAGE 66 & 67)

MIYUKI DELICA ROUND (DBR) 11/0
BEAD COLOUR KEY   QTY

⊟	DBR608 Dk Blue	■	608
L	DBR628 Med Blue	□	148

The beaded arrow symbols indicate the direction the beads should be threaded for the first row.

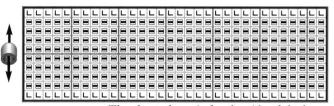

The chart above is for the side of the base.

The chart below is for the side of the lid.

This box involves decreasing in brick stitch. Decreasing, under previous decreases will create a nicer pattern.

BASE SIDE: 32 wide x 10 high

Using square stitch (method 7c so that it is rigid), work the top chart and join the short edges to make a round. Do not cut thread.

BASE BOTTOM - Brick stitch using Dark Blue.

Round 1: (24 beads) - Coming out of the centre of one of the square stitched beads, *work two, miss one*, repeat to end of round.

Round 2: (16 beads) - *work two, miss one*, repeat to end of round.

Round 3: (16 beads) - work brick stitch to end of round.

Round 4: (8 beads) - Starting with two beads, but missing the first space, * work one, miss one*, repeat to end of round.

Round 5: (4 beads) - Starting with two beads, but missing the first space, * work one, miss one*, repeat to end of round. Finish off by weaving in thread ends.

LID SIDE: 40 wide x 6 high

Using square stitch (method 7c), work the bottom chart and join the short edges together to make a round, do not cut thread.

LID TOP - Brick stitch using Dark Blue.

Round 1: (32 beads) - Coming out of the centre of one of the square stitched beads,*work four, miss one*, repeat to end of round.

Round 2: (24 beads) - *work three, miss one*, repeat to end of round.

Round 3: (24 beads).

Round 4: (16 beads) - *work two, miss one*, repeat to end of round.

Round 5: (8 beads) - Starting with two beads, but missing the first space, * work one, miss one*, repeat to end of round.

Round 6: (4 beads) - Starting with two beads, but missing the first space, * work one, miss one*, repeat to end of round. Finish off by weaving in thread ends.

You will find that the lids of the Large Round Pot (page 26), the Forget-me-not Domed Pot (page 27) and the Small Round Pot are eight beads larger in circumference than the base. I found this a good "rule of thumb" to ensure that the lid fits onto the base.

It is also a good idea to make the base first and treat is as a practice run for the brick stitch rounds, before starting on the lid. You can also double check the size of the lid by placing it onto the base after working the lid sides.

TREAT THE OUTSIDE EDGE OF THE JOINED SQUARE STITCH STRIP AS YOU WOULD LADDER STITCH WHEN WORKING THE FIRST ROUND OF TUBULAR CONCENTRIC BRICK STITCH FOR THE POTS.

When you start a round in brick stitch, always start with two beads, this hides the thread of the first stitch of the round. This step is counted as two beads in our instructions.

When finishing a round, go into the first bead again to make it sit correctly.

See brick stitch instructions on page 66 and 67.

Daffodil Amulet

Embellished with brick stitched daffodils, and a right angle weave top edging and strap.

Pictured left is the Pansy Amulet Bag from Jill Oxton's Cross Stitch & Beading Issue 54. This also uses brick stitched Pansy embellishments on the top of the square stitched bag. The chain was worked using right angle weave (one bead per side) alternating silver and gold beads. The fringe was worked using three bead picots.

Daffodils by Jill Oxton

Daffodil Amulet was worked using Delica Beads 11/0 and trimmed with 8/0 (3mm diameter) Seed Beads.

The bottom fringe uses a one bead picot and #8 Black Seed Beads and the top bag edging and strap is worked using right angle weave (RAW) embellished with 8/0 silver-lined emerald seed beads.

The Amulet was worked in square stitch using Black Nymo D thread. To add more dimension, three daffodils were then worked in brick stitch using Pumpkin Nymo D thread and secured to the front of the amulet.

Pictured left, amulet adorned with brick stitch daffodils.

Pictured right, unadorned amulet.

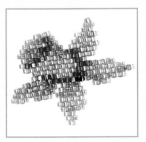 

What a difference the thread colour makes!

A perfect example are the daffodils above, which were worked in the same bead colours. The left daffodil has been worked with Pumpkin Nymo and the right daffodil with Black Nymo.

Daffodil Amulet

45 beads wide x 58 beads high

CONSTRUCTION DETAILS

AMULET: Square stitch the amulet bag first using method 7a or 7b so the beading is soft and drapey. We used Black Nymo D Thread and a No. 28 Tapestry Needle. The bead key is below. *Square stitch Instructions are on page 70.*

BRICK STITCH DAFFODILS: Work three and stitch them to the front of the bag (optional, but worth it). *I use a tiny piece of double sided tape to hold them in position before stitching down.* **Brick stitch instructions are on page 66. Use Pumpkin Nymo.**

FRINGE: Work as charted on the bottom section of daffodil chart using method 2. *Fringe instructions are on page 72.*

TOP EDGING: Work one row of RAW on the top edge, *(see page 68 Combining RAW with square stitch)*. We also filled in the RAW using #8 Silverlined Emerald Seed Beads *(see page 68)*. This was done on the wrong side, so only a glint of colour showed on the front.

STRAP: Work a 66 cm (26") RAW strap using two beads per side and fill in each side of the chain using #8 Silverlined Emerald Beads.

Note: *When filling in the chain, work one side first and then the other. I worked a combination of both and my chain became twisted, which was very pretty, but it was not consistent throughout.*

Daffodil Amulet

The bead quantity on the Amulet Key at right is for the amulet chart and fringe above. Add beads for the Brick Stitch Daffodils, strap and edging.

FOR THE STRAP AND EDGING YOU WILL NEED
480 x DBR10 Black
150 x #8 Silverlined Emerald Seed Beads to match DBR605

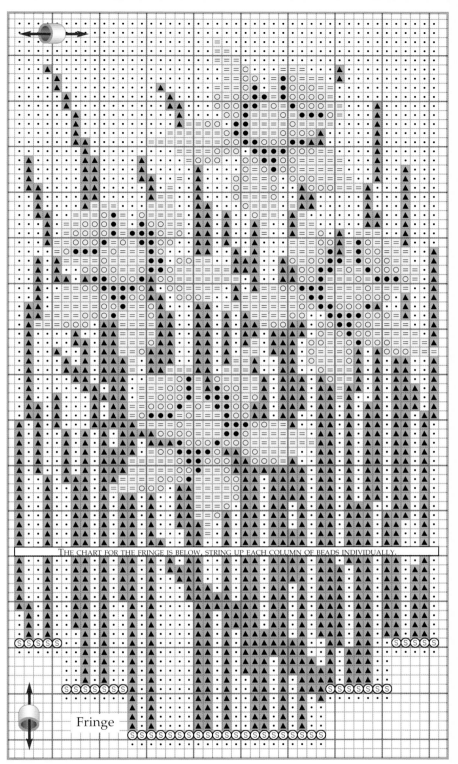

THE CHART FOR THE FRINGE IS BELOW, STRING UP EACH COLUMN OF BEADS INDIVIDUALLY.

Fringe

TO LENGTHEN THE DAFFODIL CHART, INCORPORATE THE FRINGE PATTERN.

Square Stitch Amulet

MIYUKI DELICA 11/0 KEY				QTY
DBR121	●		Dark Yellow	115
DBR100	○		Med Yellow	258
DBR233	=		Lt Yellow	414
DBR605	▲		Green	1032
DBR10	·		Black	1521
#8 Seed	Ⓢ		Black	45

Brick Stitch Daffodils

MIYUKI DELICA 11/0				QTY
DBR121	●		Dark Yellow	107
DBR100	○		Med Yellow	243
DBR233	·		Lt Yellow	307

Quantities above are for one x #1 and two x #2 brick stitch daffodils (see next page).

Brick Stitch Daffodils

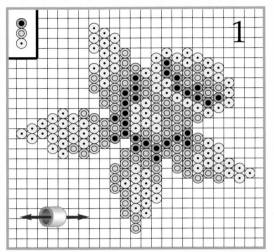

These were used on the Daffodil Amulet, but can also be used separately for brooches, hairslides, bookmarks or to decorate a box or pot.

Brick stitch instructions are on page 66.

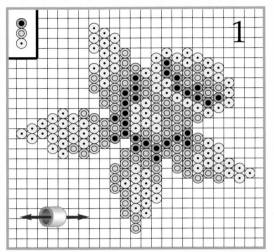

1

Above: 23 beads wide x 21 beads high

Below: 25 beads wide x 24 beads high

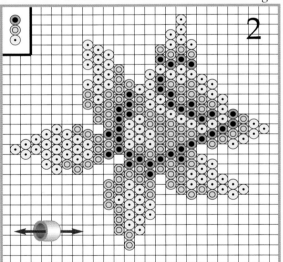

2

Miyuki Delica 11/0 Key			#1Qty	#2Qty
DBR121	●	Dark Yellow	39	39
DBR100	◉	Med Yellow	75	84
DBR233	⊙	Lt Yellow	95	106

The brick stitch daffodils were worked with Pumpkin Nymo D thread and a No. 28 Tapestry Needle.

Work one of #1 above and two of #2. Reverse one of number two before securing to the front of the amulet.

Brick Stitch Bracelets

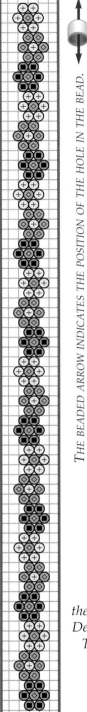

THE BEADED ARROW INDICATES THE POSITION OF THE HOLE IN THE BEAD.

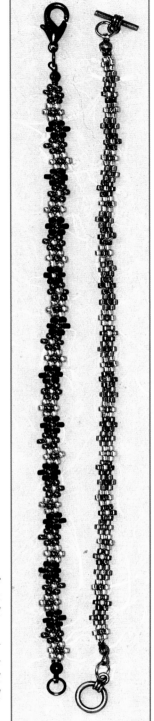

Pic: The bracelet on the right used Delica 11/0's. The bracelet on the left used Mill Hill seed beads.

Miyuki Delica		Mill Hill	11/0 Colour Key	Qty
DBR31	⊕	02011	Gold	56
DBR144	◈	00221	Bronze	64
DBR23	◼	03040	Gunmetal	48

The bracelets were worked using Pumpkin Nymo D and a No. 10 John James Blunt Beading Needle. Work bracelet around 16cm (6 ¹/₄") in length. To finish, weave thread through the beads around the outside edge of the bracelet to reinforce it.

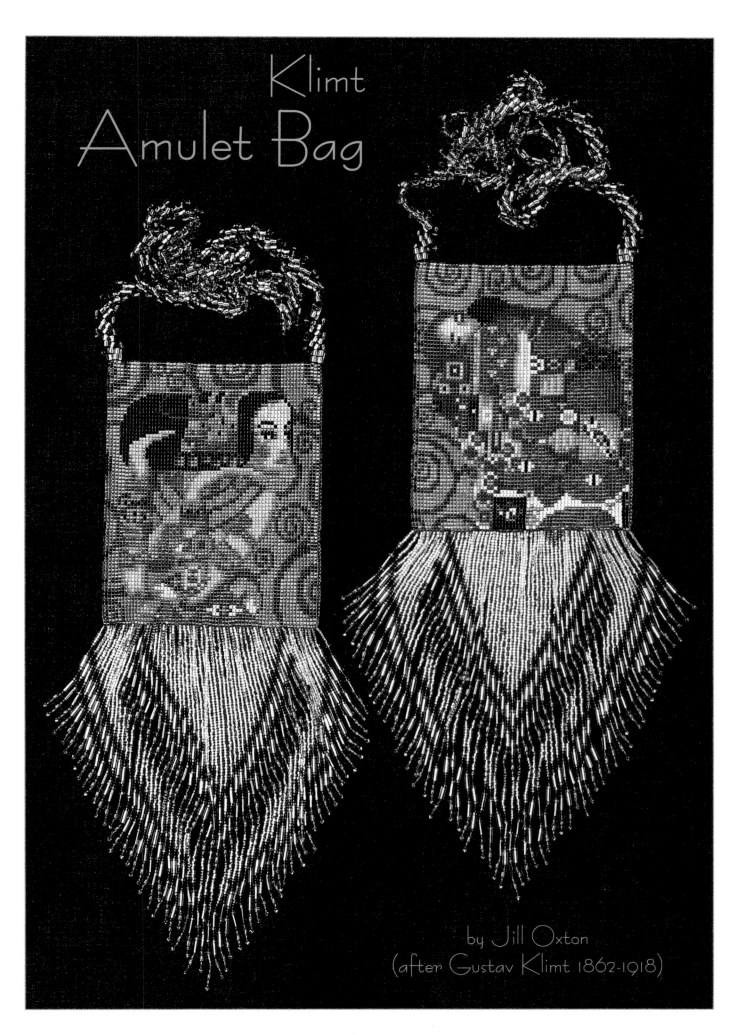

Klimt
Amulet Bag

by Jill Oxton
(after Gustav Klimt 1862-1918)

Peterburg Chain Instructions

This very attractive strap sews up very quickly and is suitable for bracelets, necklaces or straps.

Use two strands of Nymo D Thread or better yet, use one strand of Nymo F Thread (which is thicker).

Cut thread eight times longer than length of chain required and then you will not have to join on any thread. To make it easier I slash the cardboard top of the Nymo thread holder, measure off half the amount of thread and secure it in the slashed lid. Work one half of the strap, unwind the remaining length of thread from the spool and work the chain from the other end.

For the amulet bag, both ends were finished on Step 5.

Klimt Amulet Bag Strap

We used: Black Nymo F Thread and a No. 28 Tapestry Needle
No. 8 Delica DBL42 (main colour).
No. 8 Seed Beads (3mm diameter).
Silverlined Amber (accent bead).

STRAP LENGTH was 70cm (27 ¹/₂") long. Adjust this to suit yourself.

YOU WILL NEED 12 main colour and 8 accent beads per 2.5cm (1"). Multiply this by the length of strap required.

TO ATTACH THE STRAP to both edges of the bag, work out of beads A and B as indicated on the diagram. Work a very firm two drop square stitch (pink on diagram) which will hang over the existing two drop beads at the end of the strap. Anchor one pair to the front edge on one side of the bag and the second pair to the back edge on the same side of the bag. Repeat with the other end of the strap for the other side. This will give stronger support to the bag as the strap will be attached to four side edges of the bag rather than two.

Above left is Peterburg chain worked using size 8/0 Beads and Delica's. Above right, the chain is worked using 11/0 Delica's and #10 beads.

⬭ *Stopper Bead*
▯ *Main Colour*
▮ *Accent Bead*

1 Tie a stopper bead onto the end of the thread. This will be removed at the end of the beading.

Thread up five main colour beads.

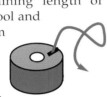

2 Take needle back through beads 2 and 3

Virtually a two drop square stitch.

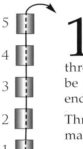

3 Pick up one accent bead and take needle back through beads 3, 2 and 1.

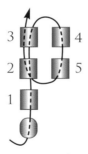

4 Pick up one accent bead at 7, go through beads 5 and 4, then pick up four main colour beads (8, 9, 10 and 11). *Repeat Steps 2, 3 and 4 until chain is the desired length, ending on Step 2 with bead 5.*

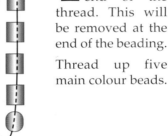

5 Repeat the pattern by taking the needle back through beads 8 and 9 (*as you did in Step 2 with beads 2 and 3*).

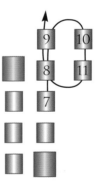

6 Pick up one accent bead and take needle back through beads 9, 8 and 7 *as you did in Step 3 with beads 3,2 and 1.*

You are now ready to add the accent bead and four main colour beads as shown in Step 4.

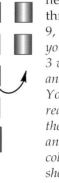

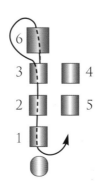

Klimt Amulet Bag

Expectation was worked for one side of the bag and Fulfilment for the other. This way you can have two different bags, but only have to make up one. These designs could also be framed or made larger, for this reason we have left the bottom section of 15 rows on the charts (which we did not work) so that you can make them longer if you wish.

The bag was worked in square stitch. The finished size of the bag and fringe (excluding chain) is 10.2cm wide x 29.5cm high (4" wide x 11⁵/₈" high) a good size for a well rounded person. My 'petite' daughter would like it with a longer strap so she could put one arm through it and wear it as a shoulder bag, but she'll just have to make her own as I am going to wear this one as an amulet bag.

These Klimt designs would also look spectacular worked in cross stitch or tapestry. Listed on this page is a suggested colour key for stranded cotton for those who would like to stitch them this way.

STITCHES USED

SQUARE STITCH- Method 7b, see pages 70 to 73.

FRINGING - chart, page 40, instructions, page 72.

PETERBURG CHAIN - instructions on page 34.

KLIMT AMULET BAG was worked using Miyuki Delica 11/0 Cylinder Beads, Pumpkin Nymo D Thread and a No. 28 Tapestry Needle. It was worked in square stitch method 7b as the square stitch should be soft and drapey.

The sides of the bag were stitched together (see page 72) and then the fringe *(see page 40)* and the strap were worked. The fringe was worked using five different sized beads in four colours.

PETERBURG CHAIN was used for the strap and because the main bead used was DBL42, a size 8/0 Delica Cylinder Bead *(which is a larger bead)* we used Black Nymo F Thread, which is thicker than D and easier than using a double strand of D). *I was not able to get Pumpkin in Nymo F, but there was no noticeable difference using black for the strap.* Using 8/0 Delica's was a quick and easy way to make a heavier strap to suit the bag.

Construction Details

Use a No. 28 Tapestry Needle or a short blunt beading needle and Pumpkin Nymo D thread. Cut your thread as long as you can manage it (1.5 to 2 metres or 1¹/₂ to 2 yards). Tie a waste bead onto the end *(this is undone later and the thread end woven into the beading, so don't tie a permanent knot).*

Turn the chart sideways and thread up the top (first) row of beads. The arrow on the chart indicates the direction of the hole in the bead.

The front and back of the amulet bag can be worked in square stitch *(see pages 70 and 72)* in two pieces and joined together at the bottom using square stitch. There must be an uneven number of rows in the combined total of the front and the back sections, so that the fringe will hang from the centre-most row of beads, not between two rows of beads. *(This is why the red line on the charts for Fulfilment and Expectation are one row out.)*

Sew the sides of the bag together, weaving all thread ends into the bag *(see page 72 for instructions).* Work the fringe **after** sewing the sides of the bag together. You will find it much easier.

Because the bag is quite heavy, I attached the strap to both the front and back and to both sides of the bag to give it extra support *(see page 36).*

ANCHOR		DMC	SUGGESTED STRANDED COTTON KEY	
403	■	310		Black
2	=	Blanc		White
10	▲	351		Dark Pink
9	▽	352		Medium Pink
914	●	3064		Dark Flesh
1008	∅	3064/950		Medium Flesh
4146	○	950		Light Flesh
1011	∪	948		Lightest Flesh
245	✖	910		Dark Green
243	✕	912		Medium Green
240	⁄	955		Light Green

ANCHOR		DMC	SUGGESTED STRANDED COTTON KEY	
122	⊟	3807		Dark Blue
121	☐	156		Medium Blue
120	∟	3747		Light Blue
906	✛	801		Brown
890	⌘	832		Medium Old Gold
891	+	834		Light Old Gold
---	−	5279		Copper Metallic
---	•	5282		Light Gold Metallic
872	▲	3041		Medium Grape
869	W	3743		Light Grape
1015	#	221		Crimson

Expectation Amulet Bag is 65 beads wide x 76 rows. Work down to the red line on the chart.

The Expectation Chart is 65 wide x 89 high. *(We left the remainder of the chart there in case you wish to work it as a framed piece in cross stitch, beads or both. See page 35 for the cross stitch key.)*

Please read construction details on page 35 before commencing.

Miyuki Delica 11/0 Key				Qty
DBR10	■	⬛	Black	510
DBR202	=	⬜	White	41
DBR62	▲		Strawberry	48
DBR106	▽		Pink	25
DBR912	●		Taupe	114
DBR256	⌀		Mauve	244
DBR205	○		Beige	305
DBR353	∪		Cream	46
DBR605	✖		Emerald	134
DBR627	✕		Green Aqua	170

Miyuki Delica 11/0 Key				Qty
DBR626	╱		Light Green	145
DBR285	⊟		Sapphire	28
DBR243	□		Med. Blue	23
DBR257	L		Light Blue	88
DBR150	✚		Brown	725
DBC121	⊕		Topaz	405
DBR623	+		Light Yellow	98
DBR144	–		Amber	147
DBR42	•		S/lined Gold	1515

Only bead to red horizontal line for Amulet Bag

Fulfilment Amulet Bag is 65 beads wide x 75 rows. Work down to the red line on the chart.

The Fulfilment Chart is 65 wide x 89 high. (*We left the remainder of the chart there in case you wish to work it as a framed piece in cross stitch or beads. See page 37 for the cross stitch key.*)

Please read construction details on page 35 before commencing.

Miyuki Delica 11/0 Key				Qty
DBR10	■	■	Black	209
DBR202	=		White	225
DBR62	▲		Strawberry	34
DBR106	▽		Pink	10
DBR912	●		Taupe	26
DBR256	∅		Mauve	47
DBR205	○		Beige	46
DBR353	∪		Cream	40
DBR605	✕		Emerald	20
DBR627	✕		Green Aqua	109
DBR626	╱		Light Green	56

Miyuki Delica 11/0 Key				Qty
DBR285	⊟		Sapphire	37
DBR257	L		Light Blue	32
DBR150	✚		Brown	570
DBC121	⊕		Topaz	406
DBR623	+		Light Yellow	145
DBR144	−		Amber	737
DBR42	•		S/lined Gold	1295
DBR799	▲		Dk. Lavender	154
DBR356	W		Lt. Lavender	113
DBR105	#		Dark Red	434

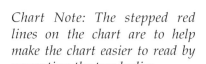

Chart Note: The stepped red lines on the chart are to help make the chart easier to read by separating the two bodies.

Fulfilment

by Jill Oxton (after Gustav Klimt 1862 - 1918)

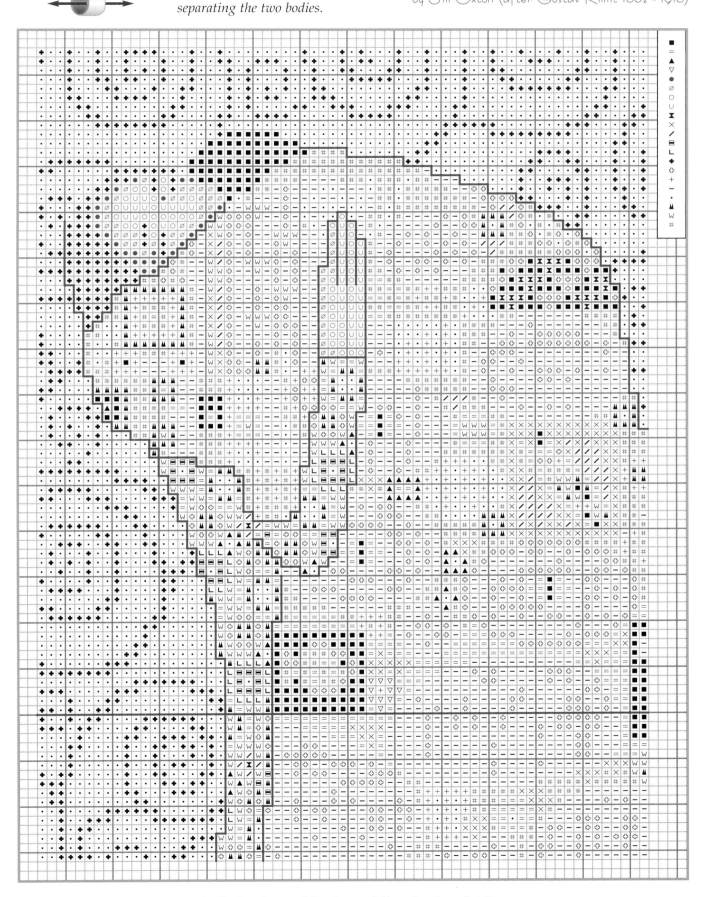

Only bead to red horizontal line for Amulet Bag

A fringe can quite often be the most expensive part of a beaded bag. Even if an embellishment bead costs only 10c, when you need a total of 318 as in this fringe, it can add up and large quantities of one particular bead can often be hard to get hold of.

For these reasons I chose inexpensive but large seed beads to use as the embellishment beads. They are the 8/0 and 6/0 on the Bead Key and were used with the 11/0 Delica Cylinder Beads, Bugle Beads and 11/0 Seed Beads in several different colours.

This gave me a very effective but inexpensive fringe, the beads were readily available and I could play around with them and use more embellishment beads in the fringe making it look more luxurious.

Size 11/0 Japanese Seed Beads and Cylinder Beads are excellent beads to use as they tend to be more uniform in size and have larger holes than other seed beads, hence we can use a No. 28 Tapestry Needle with them, which does make threading the needle so much easier.

Klimt Amulet Bag Fringe

Fringe instructions are on page 72. We used Diagram 1 and placed the fringes between the beads.

Klimt Amulet Bag Fringe

The fringe was worked using five different sized beads in four colours which complimented the golds and warm browns in the bag. We used Pumpkin Nymo D Thread and a No. 28 Tapestry Needle. You may need a finer blunt beading needle, depending on the type of embellishing beads you purchase for the fringe.

Work the fringe by stringing up each column of the chart. The beaded arrow indicates the direction of the hole in the beads. See Diagram 1 on page 72 to make the fringe.

Pull your thread taut, but not tight or you will buckle the fringes and they will not sit properly.

After every row, hold your fringe up to see that the fringes are hanging properly and are the correct length. Sometimes an extra bead or two has to be added to compensate for the more irregular shaped beads (eg the 8/0 and 6/0). Be careful with the size bugle bead used as you may need to add extra beads to allow for this. Four Delica Beads strung up were approximately the same length as one bugle bead).

Be warned, this is the largest fringe I have worked to date and I naively thought I would work this fringe in a couple of hours (or one six hour sitting at the longest). I gave up counting hours after about 12, but it probably took me 16 to 18 hours to work the fringe.

BEAD KEY FOR THE FRINGE — BEAD QTY

Code	Symbol	Description	Qty
42	•	11/0 Delica Cylinder Beads	2444
02011	O	11/0 Mill Hill Seed Beads Gold	424
02020	C	11/0 Mill Hill Seed Beads Emerald	212
82011	B	Mill Hill Medium Bugle Beads Gold 82011	212
02023	S	11/0 Mill Hill Seed Beads Brown/Dark Amber	636
	M	8/0 (3mm diameter) Silverlined Amber	212
	L	6/0 (4.5mm diameter) Seed Beads Amber	106

Approximate size of a 8/0 Bead 3mm ◉

Approximate size of a 6/0 Bead 4.5mm ◉

(With beads sitting flat and the hole in the centre of the circle.)

Approximate length of Bugle Bead 6mm ▭

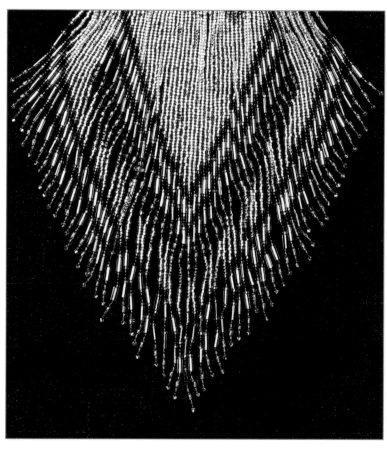

Don't stress if you can't match up the colours or the sizes of embellishing beads for a fringe (and/or a strap) exactly. Substitutions can be made, but the proportions may vary, so check each fringe length as you work it, in case you need to add extra beads to obtain a graduated length.

The Kiss, a third Klimt design will be featured in Jill Oxton's Cross Stitch & Beading Issue 58.

A Key Case

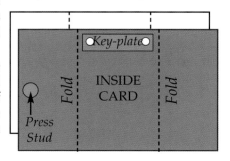

Cap & Back Rivets *are a handy item used by leather workers to attach fittings.*

A Key Case
63 high x 95 wide
Stitches used - Square Stitch

Miyuki Delica (DBR) 11/0			Qty
DBR693	•	Dark Blue	1855
DBR610	●	Dark Purple	753
DBR694	○	Med Purple	505
DBR629	–	Lt Purple	668
DBR605	▲	Med Green	1502
DBR627	▽	Lt Green	702

Black or Blue Nymo D Thread
No. 28 Tapestry Needle
5 Hook Key Plate
  47mm (1⁷/₈") wide
2 x 6mm Cap & Back Rivets
Thin Card (cereal pack thickness)
Thin Batting or felt for padding
Double-sided Tape
Small Piece of Leather *(the same size as the bar on the key plate)*
Dark Blue Fabric for Lining
Dark Blue Polyester Thread
Press Stud (or button and loop)

Work the Key Case in square stitch (method 7b so it is stretchy) using Black Nymo D Thread and a No. 28 Tapestry Needle.
You will need to turn the chart.

Construction Details:

1. Cut two pieces of card 9.5cm x 15cm wide (3 ³/₄" x 6") OR the same size as the beading.

2. Score a line 4.5cm (1³/₄") in from each side and fold. Do this for both cards.

3. Fit both cards together, fold together and trim off any overlap from the inside card. *The inside card should be cut slightly smaller than the outside card so when the case is folded the card sits correctly inside the case.*

Working with the Inside Card:

1. Centre key plate on the middle section of card. Punch holes into the card, corresponding with those on key plate.

2. Cut leather the same size as key plate and punch holes into leather to correspond with those on key plate.

3. Stick leather on centre back of card using double-sided tape and aligning all holes *(the leather is used to reinforce the card).*

4. Cover card with fabric. Mitre corners and secure the fabric edges to the back of the card using double-sided tape. Using a knitting needle, punch holes through the fabric to correspond with the holes in the card.

5. Check that all the key plate hooks are working correctly and attach the key plate to the front of the fabric covered card using cap and back rivets. Gently tap with a hammer to secure.

6. Securely sew the top section of a press stud on to the left hand side of the card using Nymo D thread.

Working with the Outside Card:

1. Cover card with batting and then fabric. Mitre corners and secure the fabric edges to the back of the card using double-sided tape.

To Assemble:

1. With wrong sides together, stick inside card onto outside card using double-sided tape.

2. Fold case to check that it is sitting correctly.

3. Neatly oversew around case, joining front and back edges together.

4. Sew the other half of press stud onto the front of the right hand flap and close case.

5. Sew the completed beading onto the outside of the case.

6. Sew a twisted cord around the outside edge if your stitching (for Step 5) is not neat (optional).

The arrow indicates the direction of the hole in the bead in relation to the chart, when working square stitch for the key case.

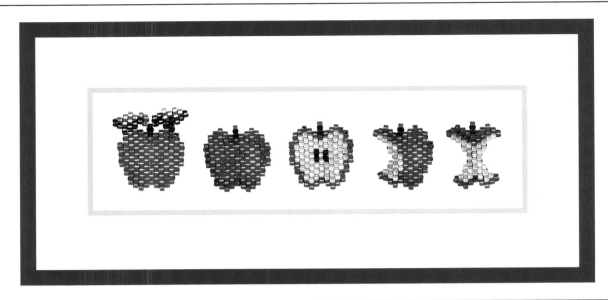

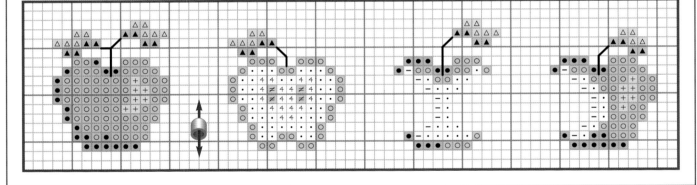

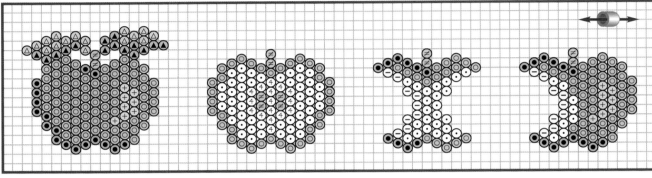

 # Apples

BY JILL OXTON

STITCHES USED

Use the top chart for Brick Stitch (see pages 66 to 67)
Use the bottom chart for Square Stitch (see pages 70 to 74)

The Apples *(pic above)* were worked in brick stitch using one strand of Wine Nymo D Thread, a No. 28 Tapestry Needle and 11/0 Miyuki Delica Beads.

Small Czech Leaves can also be attached to the apples using 28 gauge wire or thread.

The apples can be used for gift tags, get well cards, bookmarks and charms on a bracelet or wine glass.

MIYUKI DELICA 11/0 KEY				QTY BRICK	QTY SQUARE
DBR 605	▲		Medium Green	15	20
DBR 627	△		Light Green	16	24
DBR 654	●		Matt Dark Red	41	44
DBR 602	O		S/L Dark Red	178	148
DBR 682	+		S/L Orange	16	13
DBR 201	·		White	82	65
DBR 80	−		Light Mauve	18	16
DBR 764	≠		Brown	12	4
DBR 203	4		Light Beige	16	8

Striped Possum

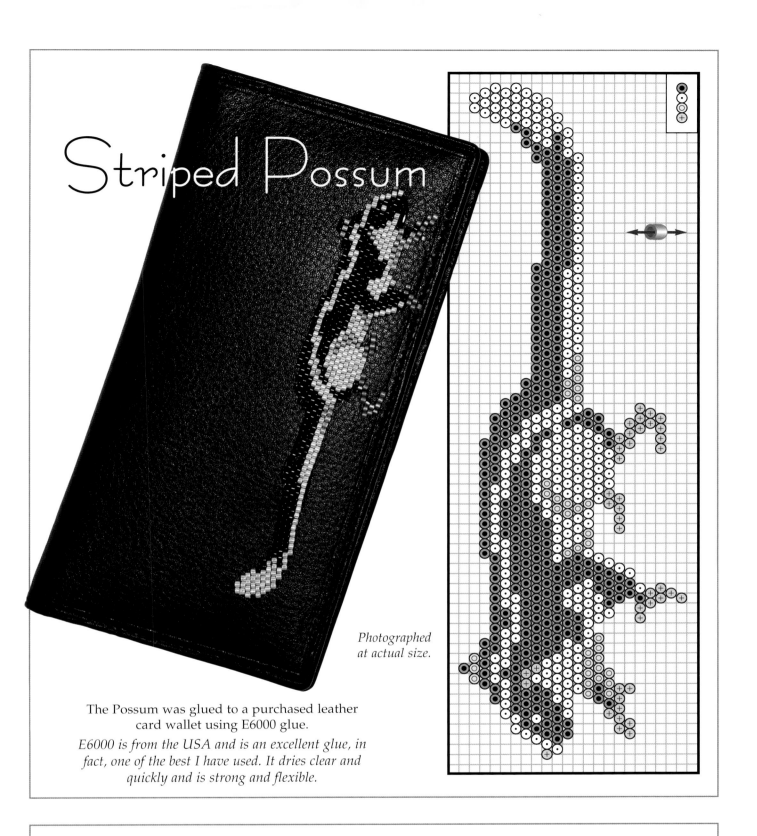

Photographed at actual size.

The Possum was glued to a purchased leather card wallet using E6000 glue.

E6000 is from the USA and is an excellent glue, in fact, one of the best I have used. It dries clear and quickly and is strong and flexible.

Striped Possum

BY JILL OXTON

STITCHES USED

Brick Stitch (see pages 66 to 67)

Striped Possum was worked in brick stitch using one strand of Black Nymo D Thread, a No. 28 Tapestry Needle and 11/0 Miyuki Delica Cylinder Beads.

MIYUKI DELICA 11/0 KEY				QTY
DBR 10	●	■	Black	283
DBR 201	·	□	White	233
DBR 80	○	▨	Lt. Mauve	36
DBR 191	⊕	▨	Dk. Flesh	37

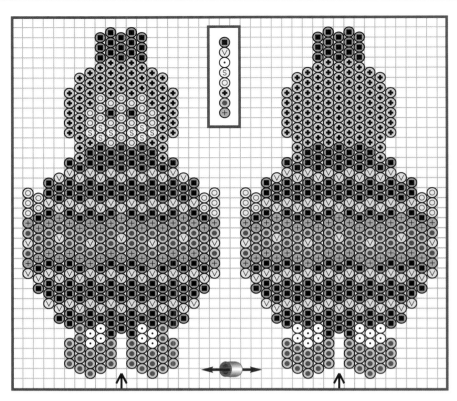

*Shown
at actual size.*

Xmas Bauble BY JILL OXTON

STITCHES USED

LADDER STITCH (SEE PAGE 66)

BRICK STITCH (SEE PAGE 66)

XMAS BAUBLE was worked in brick stitch using one strand of Wine Nymo D Thread, a No. 28 Tapestry Needle.

The black arrow on the chart indicates our starting point for ladder stitch. The beaded arrow indicates the direction the hole in the bead should lie.

Two sides (a front and back) were worked. Join both pieces together by placing on top of each other and stitching through the beads on the edge.

Stitch one side edge together and place a tiny pinch of fibre fill or cotton wool inside the head and body to pad it slightly, too much and you will have a gap between the pieces. Use a match-stick or

			BAUBLE	MARBLE
MIYUKI DELICA 11/0 KEY			**QTY**	**QTY**
DBR 10		Black	300	236
DBR 31		Gold	138	93
DBR 202		White	20	0
DBR 207		Peach	8	8
DBR 205		Beige	21	21
DBC 121		Topaz	141	141
DBR 683		D. Ruby	140	20
DBR 605		Emerald	76	8
1 x Bead Tip				

toothpick to push the wadding into the correct place and then continue stitching the front and back together.

Xmas Marble

is a combination of the Xmas Bauble and the Beaded Marble Posy on page 55.

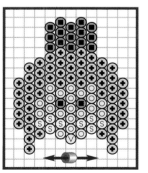

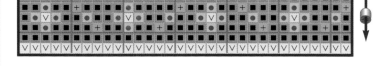

STITCHES USED

SQUARE STITCH PAGE 70, SQUARE TO BRICK PAGE 75 & BRICK STITCH PAGE 66

XMAS MARBLE was stitched using one strand of Wine Nymo D Thread, a No. 28 Tapestry Needle and 11/0 Miyuki Delica Cylinder Beads. You will also need one 17mm diameter marble *(see page 55)* and some foil.

Using brick stitch work the head of the Xmas Bauble, chart top left. The back of the head is all Topaz except for the hat.

Work chart bottom left in square stitch, method 7c and join together to make a round. *Adjust size to fit around marble if needed.*

continued on page 47

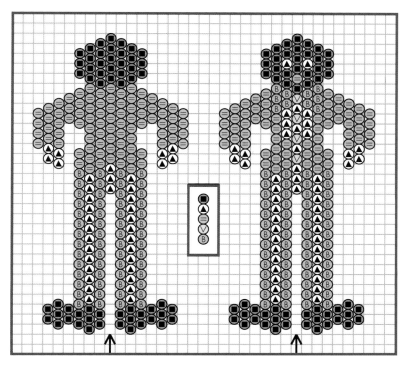

My Golli

Shown at actual size.

The arrow indicates the direction of the hole in the bead in relation to the chart when working brick stitch .

MIYUKI DELICA 11/0 KEY			QTY
DBR 10	■	Black	175
DBR 201	▲	White	85
DBR 723	=	Red	149
DBR 31	V	Gold	4
DBR 726	B	Blue	122

My Golli

BY MARGARET LEYLAND

STITCHES USED

LADDER STITCH (SEE PAGE 66)
BRICK STITCH (SEE PAGES 66)
FRINGING (SEE PAGE 72)

Golli was worked using one strand of Black Nymo D Thread, a No. 28 Tapestry Needle and 11/0 Miyuki Delica Beads.

Cut your thread about 2 metres (72") long. This should be long enough for one side, without any joins.

The black arrow on the chart indicates our starting point for ladder stitch. The beaded arrow indicates the direction the hole in the beads should lie.

Two sides (a front and back) were worked. Join both pieces together by placing on top of each other and stitching through the beads on the edge.

Stitch one side and then place a tiny pinch of fibre fill or cotton wool inside the head and body to pad it slightly, too much and you will have a gap between the pieces. Use a toothpick to push the wadding into the correct place and then continue stitching the front and back together.

Finish off by adding about twenty very tight fringes (DBR10 black) around the outside of the head for the hair. We did three bead fringes for all except for the first and last fringes, where we used two beads (just above the shoulders).

Xmas Marble

continued from page 46

Work brick stitch on the upper and lower edges of the square stitched round, using a marble as a form *(as detailed on page 55)*.

Round 1: (24 beads) - **Using black beads,** *work three, miss 1*, repeat to end of round.

Round 2: (24 beads) - Using black beads, *work brick stitch to end of round.*

Round 3: (16 beads) - Using gold beads *work two, miss 1*, repeat to end of round.

Round 4: (16 beads) - Using black beads, *work brick stitch to end of round.*

Round 5: (8 beads) - Using black beads, *work one, miss 1*, repeat to end of round.

ROUND 6 FOR LOWER EDGE ONLY: (4 beads) - Using gold beads, *work one, miss one*, four times. Weave in thread end.

ROUND 6: FOR UPPER EDGE ONLY (8 beads) - Using gold beads, *work one, miss 1*, repeat to end of round.

Attach the head to the top of the marble and weave in thread ends securely.

Rose Amulet Bag

BY DI NOYCE

This delicate little Amulet Bag was worked in square stitch in a strip and then joined at the sides (see page 72). If you start working from the flat edge of the bag, the fold over flap involves decreasing only. The simple, but elegant chain uses the same colour beads as used for the bag, plus Delica 8/0 silver-lined crystal as an accent bead. Use two strands of Nymo D thread for the chain. The red lines on the chart indicate the fold lines for the top and bottom edges.

STITCHES USED

SQUARE STITCH SEE PAGES 70 TO 74
(method 7b so it drapes nicely)

YOU WILL NEED:

Silver Nymo D Thread (to match the main colour bead used).

No. 10 Blunt Beading Needle.

ROSE AMULET BAG KEY

Japanese Cylinder Beads 11/0

49 BEADS HIGH X 136 BEADS WIDE.

DELICA 11/0		COLOUR KEY	QTY
DBR690	■	Dark Green	253
DBR238	☐	Medium Green	101
DBR112	L	Light Green	265
DBR105	●	Dark Pink	858
DBR62	◉	Medium Pink	272
DBR106	○	Light Pink	264
DBR71	∞	Lightest Pink	99
DBR41	·	Silverlined Crystal	4673

THE CHAIN 81CM 32" *(adjust to fit)*			
DBL41		8/0 Silverlined Crystal	50
DBR41		Silverlined Crystal	200
DBR106		Dark Pink	100
DBR62		Medium Pink	100
DBR105		Light Pink	50

DBR41
DBR41
DBL41
DBR41
DBR41
DBR106
DBR62
DBR105
DBR62
DBR106
DBR41
DBR41
DBL41
DBR41
DBR41

Pattern Repeat to desired length.

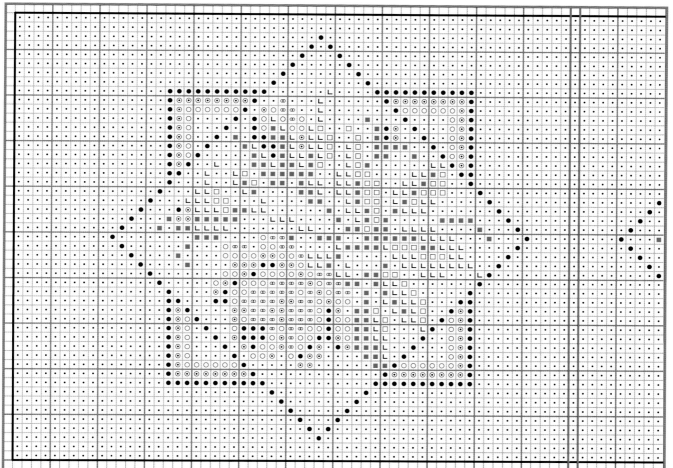

CHART CONTINUED BELOW.

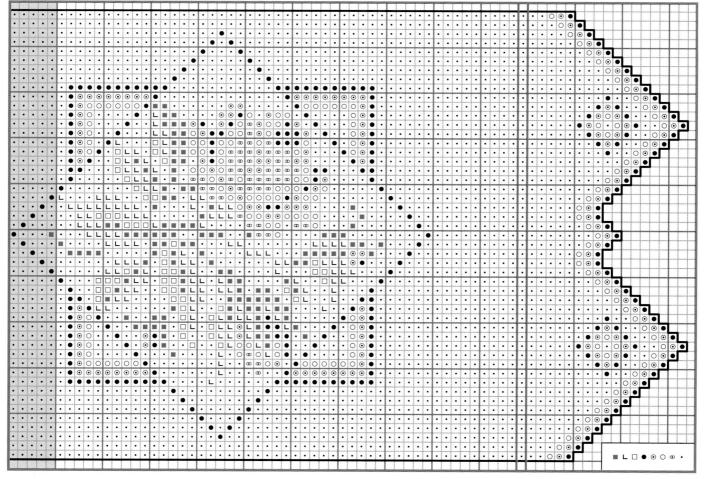

Viola Needle Case

BY JILL OXTON

BASE: 30 high x 30 wide

LID: 6 high x 30 wide

STITCHES USED

SQUARE STITCH - PAGE 70
CHANGING THE DIRECTION OF SQUARE STITCH - PAGE 73
SQUARE STITCH WORKED IN THE ROUND
(this is worked from the outside edge in to the centre).

Chart above - base

Chart left - lid

Work in square stitch.

The beading was set onto a turned wooden needlecase.

Square stitch was worked for the side of the base and lid in a flat piece and then sewn onto the needlecase. The bottom of the base and top of the lid were closed up using square stitch worked from the outside edge in to the centre. The direction of the square stitch was changed for this. See the diagram on page 73.

Twelve fringes were hung from the centre of the base using various sized and shaped beads incorporating the colours used in the design.

Hint: If the lid of your needlecase is loose, paint the inside of the lid with one or two coats of clear nail polish to tighten it up.

WE USED:

MIYUKI DELICA (DBR) 11/0   QTY

			QTY
DBR610	▲	Dark Purple	30
DBR923	▽	Med Purple	34
DBR249	∧	Lt Purple	42
DBR629	—	Ltst Purple	14
DBR112	▤	Med Green	68
DBR60	▢	Lt Green	119
DBR331	◉	Dull Gold	52
DBR310	▢	Dull Black	827

Wooden Needlecase - *5.8cm high x 1.2cm diameter (2 $^1/_4$" x $^1/_2$").*
Black Nymo D Thread
No. 28 Tapestry Needle
Kikusui Double sided Tape

NEEDLECASE BASE:

1   Work top chart, place around wooden needlecase and square stitch the side edges together.

2   *Now work the bottom of base using circular square stitch along the bottom edge of the square stitch. The beads will sit in a different direction, to do this see diagram on page 73.*

ROUND 1 - USES 24 BLACK BEADS

Reverse direction of square stitch and decrease. Work 4, miss 1 all around.

ROUND 2 - USES 24 BLACK BEADS

Square stitch in all of the beads.

ROUND 3 - USES 12 BLACK BEADS

Decrease round. Work 1, miss 1 all around, then run thread through these beads several times and pull taut to tighten up the round.

ROUND 4 - USES 3 BLACK BEADS

Decrease round. Close up the hole in the centre by working 1, missing 3 , all around. Finish off by weaving ends into beading.

NECK: USES 25 BLACK BEADS:

On the top edge of base reverse direction of square stitch and decrease. Work 5, miss 1 all around.

Run the thread through all of the beads of this round twice and finish off thread ends by weaving them into the beading.

NEEDLECASE LID:

1   Work bottom chart and attach this onto the lid of needlecase using doublesided tape. Square stitch the side edges together.

Work the top of the lid the same as for the base.

FRINGES

Attach fringes from the centre of the base using a separate piece of thread.

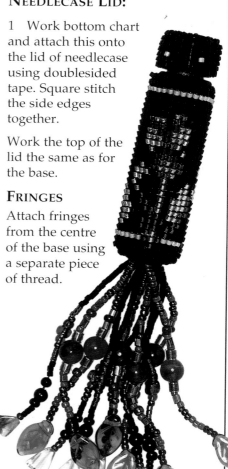

 # Cherry Pocket Brooch

BY JILL OXTON

STITCHES USED

SQUARE STITCH (SEE PAGES 70)
RIGHT ANGLE WEAVE (RAW)(SEE PAGE 68)
FRINGING - 3 BEAD PICOT (SEE PAGE 72)

Cherry Pocket Brooch was worked in square stitch method 7b using one strand and right angle weave (RAW) using two strands of Black Nymo D Thread, a No. 28 Tapestry Needle and 11/0 Miyuki Delica Cylinder Beads.

The flap of the bag was worked in square stitch and the remainder was worked in RAW using two beads per side, with DBR10 Black. The lower edge of the flap was fringed using a three bead picot with DBR10 Black.

A three hole brooch bar was sewn onto the back of the bag using Nymo D thread.

CONSTRUCTION DETAILS

Cut your thread as long as you can manage it and work the flap (front) of the bag in square stitch as charted. *(Ignore red squares and treat the 'black square in circle' symbol as a black square.)* On the top of the bag work 10 RAW's as shown on the chart.

The *'red square in a circle'* symbol indicates the first row of RAW, work three sides of this and pick up the fourth side (the other two stitches) from the top row of the square stitch *(where indicated on the chart by the 'black square in a circle').*

Work 26 rows of RAW. Fold the RAW over so the front of the bag section is 12 RAW high and join together with the back section of RAW, using RAW.

The Fringe was worked using a Three Bead Picot. Fringes are indicated with a red line on the chart. The first fringe comes out at A as indicated on the chart and uses three beads. The second fringe (B) uses four beads. Third and subsequent fringes use five beads. Repeat B and A for the last two fringes.

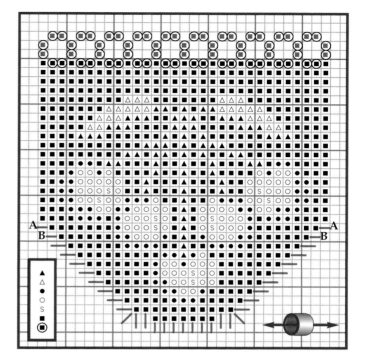

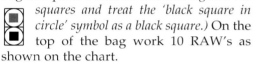

MIYUKI DELICA 11/0 KEY			QTY
DBR 605	▲	Medium Green	70
DBR 916	△	Light Green	26
DBR 654	●	Matt Dark Red	74
DBR 602	○	S/L Dark Red	85
DBR 682	S	S/L Orange	10
DBR 10	■	Black	469
DBR 10	◉	Black *RAW*	1290

The arrow on the chart indicates the direction of the hole in the bead.

You get approximately 170 to 180 beads per gram of Miyuki Delica 11/0's.

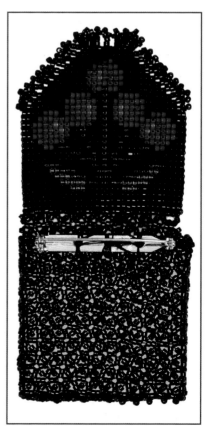

Daffodil

BY JILL OXTON

DAFFODIL USES LADDER STITCH AND BRICK STITCH.

MIYUKI DELICA ROUND 11/0		QTY
DBR65	Dark Yellow	7
DBR233	Medium Yellow	76
DBR232	Light Yellow	16

Pumpkin Nymo D thread
No. 28 Tapestry Needle
1 Knitting Needle (see note below)

CUT THREAD 1 METRE (40") LONG

DAFFODIL BELL (Medium Yellow)

Row 1: (8 beads) Work Ladder Stitch.

Row 2: (8 beads) Brick Stitch.

Row 3 Decrease Row: (6 beads) Work 2, miss 1, work 3, miss 1, work 1.

Row 4: (6 beads) Brick Stitch.

JOIN SIDES TOGETHER to form a round (DIAG 1) and weave thread back to Row 1.

DIAG 1

THE FRILL ON BELL (Light Yellow)

Row 5: (8 beads) *We are converting to Peyote Stitch and the beads will eventually be at a different angle to the brick stitch beads (DIAG 2).*

*Bring needle through centre of a bead on Row 1, *add 1 bead and go back down through the same bead, then come out of the next bead* and repeat from * to * seven times.

DIAG 2

Row 6: (8 beads) Peyote Stitch. This row will straighten up the beads of Row 5 (DIAG 3).

DIAG 3

Run thread though peyote stitch beads several times and pull taut.

Weave thread back down to the base of the bell, coming out of the centre of a bead.

After the bell was worked I found it easier to place the beading onto a knitting needle to hold it, while working the petals.

DAFFODIL PETALS (Medium Yellow)

Coming out of the centre of one of the base beads, Brick Stitch a petal. *Work the first row of each petal with a loose tension so the petals will bend at a 45º angle. I placed my thumb nail between the base and the first row of the petal to achieve this.*

Row 1: (2 beads) Brick Stitch.

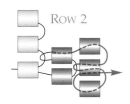

ROW 1

Row 2: (3 beads) Brick Stitch.

ROW 2

Row 3: (2 beads) Brick Stitch.

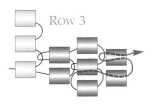

ROW 3

Row 4: (1 bead). Come out of centre of bead on row 4 add one bead and then go into the next bead.

Run thread around the entire petal and pull taut. Take thread through the centre of the bead you came out of and then come out of the centre of the bead beside it to work the next petal. A total of six petals should be worked.

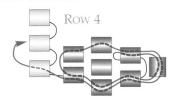

ROW 4

Now, to help petals sit properly, weave around all 12 beads of the first row of petals, joining them together.

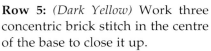

Row 5: (Dark Yellow) Work three concentric brick stitch in the centre of the base to close it up.

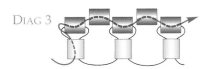

STAMEN (Dark Yellow)

Take needle and thread through the centre of the base, add four beads and go back down through the first three beads to form a single fringe, taking needle and thread back through the centre of the base.

Weave other end back through to base and knot both ends together.

Leave the thread ends on the daffodil until you decide what to do with them as they can be used to attach the daffodil to an item.

Daffodil Vase

A daffodil was set onto a miniature vase which was beaded around a marble using a combination of square stitch and brick stitch.

STITCHES USED:

SQUARE STITCH *page 70*
SQUARE STITCH TO
    BRICK STITCH *page 75*
BRICK STITCH *page 66*

YOU WILL NEED

1 GLASS MARBLE *no larger than 21mm in diameter.*

FOIL CHOCOLATE WRAPPER.

BLUE NYMO D THREAD

678 (4GMS) OF DBR923 MIYUKI DELICA 11/0

21 mm

THE CENTRE OF VASE AND BASE

ROWS 1 TO 11: Square Stitch a strip **11 beads high x 36 beads wide**. *This should be wide enough to fit around the marble when joined.*

Join the short edges of the strip together. Wrap the marble with the foil *(with the excess foil at the base)* and place into round to check fit, then remove. **It should be a snug fit.**

ON ONE EDGE OF THE BEADED STRIP, WORK ROWS 12 TO 16: *Same as rows 24 to 28 of Basic Fish pattern on page 58.*

ROW 17: *Uses 4 beads and is a decrease row.* ***Add 2 beads, miss two spaces and Brick Stitch 1 bead, *miss one space, Brick stitch 1 bead*, twice,** then brick stitch into first bead of round and weave in thread end.

THE TOP OF VASE AND NECK

Insert foil wrapped marble with excess foil at the base. This will flatten down and create a flat base for the vase, keeping the vase stable.

ON THE OTHER EDGE OF THE BEADED STRIP, WORK ROWS 18 TO 19: *Same as rows 24 to 25 of Basic Fish pattern on page 58.*

ROW 20: *Repeat row 25 of Basic Fish pattern.*

ROW 21: *Uses 18 beads and is a decrease row.* ***Brick stitch 3 beads, miss 1 bead*,** repeat to end of round.

ROWS 22 TO 24: *Uses 18 beads.* Brick stitch all around.

ROW 25: *Uses 36 beads.* Work a two drop brick stitch all around. Weave in thread end and attach daffodil just below the neck of the vase, checking that the vase is not top heavy.

Potted Daffodil

A daffodil was set into a miniature clay pot using E6000 glue and the top sprinkled with brown seed beads. We made our own "stump work" leaves as I couldn't find any beads suitable for daffodil leaves.

YOU WILL NEED

To make the stem and leaves of the daffodil
26 OR 28 GAUGE WIRE
102 CM (40") OF GREEN STRANDED COTTON

TO MAKE THE STEM

Cut a piece of wire 16 cm (6.5") long, bend in half and thread this through the centre of the bell of the beaded daffodil.

Cut a piece of green stranded cotton 102cm (40") long. Pull one thread from the stranded cotton and fold in half, threading the ends through the eye of a No.28 tapestry needle.

Secure the thread to the top of the wire (DIAG. 1) by taking the needle through the loop of the tail and tightly weave the thread over and under the wire until the stem is the desired length (DIAG. 2). Our stem was about 3cm (1.25") in length. Firmly secure the thread end in the weaving. Leave excess wire at the base.

DIAG. 1

DIAG. 2

TO MAKE THE LEAVES

We made three leaves between 2.5cm (1") to 3cm (1.25") in length.

Squeeze the end of the wire to a point and secure the thread to the top of the wire. Weave thread over and under the wire until the stem is the desired length and finish off as for stem. Leave the thread on the end of one of the leaves.

TO FINISH OFF

Arrange the stem and leaves and twist the wire at the base firmly. Wrap green stranded cotton around twisted wire a few times, secure and cut thread. Wrap the excess wire into a coil to act as a base and glue this inside the flower pot with a generous amount of glue.

To finish off, we sprinkled brown seed beads on top of the glue to represent soil. Use inexpensive 11/0 or 15/0 beads for this.

Forget-me-not BY JILL OXTON

STITCHES USED
CIRCULAR CONCENTRIC BRICK STITCH (SEE PAGE 67).
BRICK STITCH (SEE PAGE 66).

DIAGRAM 1

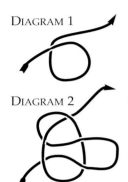

DIAGRAM 2

SLIP KNOT

1. Make a loop with the tail end on top. (Diag 1).

2. Pull a loop from the tail end through the loop. (Diag 2).

3. Holding both ends of thread, draw the loop up, tightening the knot.

4. Pull the tail end a little to check the slip knot will close.

---

1 Cut your thread about 1 metre (40") long and make a slip knot with the tail end, making sure the tail slides through the knot. *See slip knot diagram above.*

Make a round of five beads around the slip knot (see instructions on page 67).

2 **Petal 1st Row:** Pick up two beads and work one brick stitch.

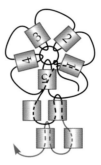

3 **Petal 2nd Row:** Pick up two beads and work one brick stitch.

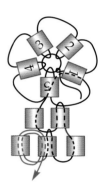

4 Work a ladder stitch next to the brick stitch just worked. Weave back, to exit from the middle bead.

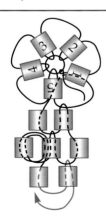

5 **Petal 3rd Row:** Pick up two beads and work a brick stitch.

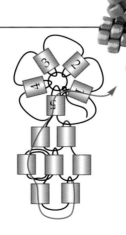

6 Weave to next bead of round and repeat steps 2 to 5. *Repeat steps 2 to 5 until five petals have been worked.*

7 Use a contrasting size 8 seed bead for the flower centre. This can also be used to attach the Forget-me-not to an item.

Colour Variation

By using two or more colours you can get many variations.

Our examples show two colour variations (using a light and dark shade of pink and blue).

Forget-me-not Posies

STITCHES USED
SQUARE STITCH (SEE PAGE 70)
BRICK STITCH (SEE PAGE 67)
SQUARE STITCH TO BRICK STITCH
(SEE PAGE 75)
FORGET-ME-NOTS (PAGE 54)

The Posies can be worked using any colours, we have worked a pink, blue and metallic version. The flowers do stand out more from the base if they are worked using a light and a dark shade of a particular colour, as used for the pink and blue posies, or in a single contrasting colour, as used for the metallic version.

PINK POSY
MIYUKI DELICA ROUND (DBR) 11/0

BEAD COLOUR KEY	QTY
DBR106 Dark Pink	474
DBR62 Light Pink	50
No. 8 Yellow Seed Beads	3
Glass Leaves	3
17mm diameter Marble	1
Thin Metallic Foil Wrapper	1
Wine Nymo D Thread	
No. 28 Tapestry Needle	

BLUE POSY
MIYUKI DELICA ROUND (DBR) 11/0

BEAD COLOUR KEY	QTY
DBR285 Dark Blue	454
DBR257 Light Blue	80
DBR721 Yellow	3
Glass Leaves	3
17mm diameter Marble	1
Thin Metallic Foil Wrapper	1
Blue Nymo D Thread	
No. 28 Tapestry Needle	

METALLIC POSY
MIYUKI DELICA ROUND (DBR) 11/0

BEAD COLOUR KEY	QTY
DBR29 Med. Bronze Iris	424
DBR331 Dull Gold	120
DBR10 Black	3
Glass Leaves	3
17mm diameter Marble	1
Thin Metallic Foil Wrapper	1
Wine Nymo D Thread	
No. 28 Tapestry Needle	

We worked three Forget-me-nots in colours to match the base and attached them to the top of each beaded marble with thread, adding the three glass leaves at the same time.

POSY SIDE 32 wide x 7 high:
Using square stitch *(method 7b so that it is stretchy)*, thread up seven beads and work 32 rows using the main colour. Join the short edges together to make a round. Do not cut the thread.

POSY BASE - *Work from one of the edges of the square stitched round, brick stitch using the main colour bead.*

Round 1: (You will use 24 beads) - **Brick Stitch three, miss one**, repeat to end of round.

Round 2: (24 beads) - *Work brick stitch to end of round.*

Round 3: (16 beads) - **Work two, miss one**, repeat to end of round.

Round 4: (16 beads) - *Work brick stitch to end of round.*

Round 5: (8 beads) - **Work one, miss one**, repeat to end of round.

Round 6: (4) beads - **Work one, miss one**, four times and weave thread to the top of the square stitch side.

POSY TOP - **Insert foil wrapped marble** into base and repeat Rounds 1 to 6 to close up the top, also see note below.

Note: If after round 5 it does not look like round 6 will cover the marble, work another round of eight beads.

Always start a brick stitch round with two beads (this is also counted as two beads).

The posies involve decreasing in brick stitch. Decreasing, under previous decreases will create a nicer pattern.

Small marbles were used as the forms for the posies. When raiding my son's marble collection I discovered that there are many different sizes of marbles, and used those that fitted easily inside the joined square stitched side without stretching it. Our marble was 17mm in diameter.

17 mm

Wrap a small marble (see note above) in thin metallic foil (the type chocolate liqueurs come in is perfect, we used Cherry Liqueurs). Use the whole wrapper and mold the excess foil onto the base of the marble. This has several purposes. It makes the marble a desirable colour and builds up the marble to the right size.

Keeping the excess foil on the base helps the marble to sit properly. Gently push down on the marble and this will flatten and mold the excess foil around the base beads, forming a small flat base.

When making the metallic version, I worked the flowers in the same colour as the base, but they did not stand out at all. Rather than unpick, which I hate, I saved the piece by painting the flowers with gold metallic acrylic paint and was very pleased with the result.

The centre beads were painted black to contrast with the flower. The key is correct!

Sweet Violets

BY JILL OXTON

Brick stitch flat and 3D Violets for embellishing boxes, earrings, bracelets, necklaces, brooches and decorating cards, gift tags and amulet bags.

STITCHES USED

LADDER STITCH AND BRICK STITCH.

The arrow on the charts shows the first row we worked. ⟶

The beaded arrow indicates the direction of the hole in the bead when working brick stitch.

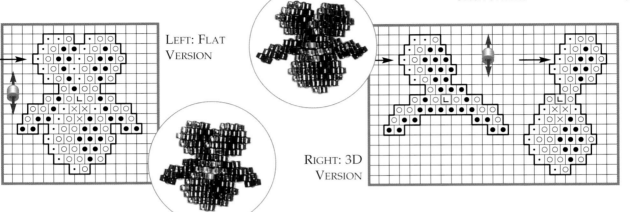

LEFT: FLAT VERSION

RIGHT: 3D VERSION

PURPLE VIOLET

MIYUKI DELICA ROUND 11/0			QTYF	QTY3D
DBR610	●	Dark Purple	34	44
DBR923	O	Medium Purple	43	45
DBR249	·	Light Purple	19	19
DBR100	L	Medium Yellow	1	2
DBR232	×	Light Yellow	3	3

We used blue Nymo D thread.

WHITE VIOLET

MIYUKI DELICA ROUND 11/0			QTYF	QTY3D
DBR231	●	Dark White	34	44
DBR209	O	Medium White	43	45
DBR351	·	Light White	19	19
DBR100	L	Medium Yellow	1	2
DBR232	×	Light Yellow	3	3

We used silver Nymo D thread.

BLUE VIOLET

MIYUKI DELICA ROUND 11/0			QTYF	QTY3D
DBR285	●	Dark Blue	34	44
DBR243	O	Medium Blue	43	45
DBR257	·	Light Blue	19	19
DBR100	L	Medium Yellow	1	2
DBR707	×	Darkest Blue	3	3

We used blue Nymo D thread.

The violets were worked in brick stitch using a No. 28 tapestry needle and can be worked either flat or in two pieces which gives a more three dimensional effect.

A size 11/0 or 10/0 yellow seed bead can be added to the centre of the violet after the brick stitching has been completed.

For a 3D Violet, work the violet in two sections and then join together through the (**L** - Medium Yellow) centre beads as indicated on the diagram below. A seed bead can also be attached at this point.

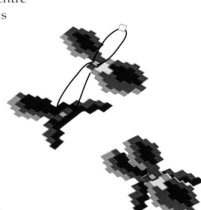

You may like to place a stitch either side of the **L** symbol on the base petals to stop the top petals twisting around. The 3D Violet is by far the more fiddly and time consuming option, but I think it is worth it.

Finding Nymo

The Basic Beaded Fish BY JILL OXTON

The centre section of the body is worked in a strip using square stitch, which is then joined into a round and placed around a glass marble.

Using this method I found it easier to incorporate a pattern and/or texture on the centre strip. We used a mixture of size 11/0 Delica's and Japanese Seed Beads for this on the Pink Fish on page 62 and the Purple Fish pictured on page 64.

The head and tail end were worked using brick stitch. The fins were worked in square stitch, directly onto the beaded body and the eyes and gills are seed bead embellishments, sewn onto the completed body.

STITCHES USED
SQUARE STITCH SEE PAGE 70
BRICK STITCH SEE PAGE 66

YOU WILL NEED:
Japanese Cylinder Beads Size 11/0
   approximately 1000 = 6gms
2 x Size 6/0 Seed Beads *(for the eyes)*
Size 12/0 or 15/0 Japanese Seed Beads
   (1 gm for gills and embellishing if desired)
Nymo D Thread
   to match the main colour bead (we used Silver)
John James No. 10 Blunt Beading Needle
1 x Glass marble *(21mm diameter, see diag on page 53)*
2 x Thin Silver Foil Chocolate Wrappers

Depending on the size of the marble used, you may have to pad the marble with metallic foil or adjust the with of the strip for rows 1 to 11.

THE BODY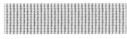

ROWS 1 TO 11: Square stitch a strip **11 beads high x 36 beads wide**. *This should be wide enough to fit around the marble when joined.* **We used the chart on page 59.**

Join the short edges of the strip together and place over the marble, this should be a snug fit.

You will now change to brick stitch and work in the round for the end of the fish body. **We used Purple DBR249.**

ROW 12: *Uses 30 beads and is a decrease row.* **Brick stitch 5 beads miss 1 bead**, repeat to end of round. *If you have worked rows 1 to 11 a different width, evenly decrease until you end up with 30 beads for this round.*

ROW 13: *Uses 30 beads.* Brick stitch all around.

ROW 14: *Uses 30 beads.* Brick stitch all around.

ROW 15: *Uses 24 beads and is a decrease row.* **Brick stitch 4 beads, miss 1 bead**, repeat to end of the round.

ROW 16: *Uses 24 beads.* Brick stitch all around.

ROW 17: *Uses 20 beads and is a decrease row.* **Brick stitch 5 beads, miss 1 bead**, repeat to end of the round.

ROW 18: *Uses 20 beads.* Brick stitch to end of round.

ROW 19: *Uses 16 beads and is a decrease row.* **Brick stitch 4 beads, miss 1 bead**, repeat to end of round.

ROW 20: *Uses 16 beads.* Brick stitch to end of round.

ROW 21: *Uses 12 beads and is a decrease row.* **Brick stitch 3 beads, miss 1 bead**, repeat to end of round.

ROW 22: *Uses 12 beads.* Brick stitch to end of round.

ROW 23: *Uses 8 beads and is a decrease row.* **Brick stitch 2 beads, miss 1 bead**, repeat to end of round.

CONSTRUCTING THE TAIL (*Use Caudal Fin chart on page 59.*) The tail is worked in square stitch on the end of row 23. Pinch the tail end so it folds in half horizontally or vertically and change the angle of the beading if necessary, so you can work the square stitch centred along one edge of the round. (*See page 73 Changing Direction of Beads, for method*). This is the first row of the Caudal Fin chart.

The centre of the tail should line up with the spine line of the fish. (Note the chart markings on the square stitched strip charts.) When the tail has been worked, weave thread ends in securely and cut.

Remove the marble from the beading and pack the tail end of the beading with one or two of the foil wrappers, reinsert marble and pinch the back of the body into a pleasing shape.

CONSTRUCTING THE HEAD

You should now move to the other end of body next to the first row worked. **We used Aqua DBR166 for the head.**

ROW 24: *Uses 30 beads and is a decrease row.* **Brick stitch 5 beads miss 1 bead**, repeat to end of round. *If you have worked rows 1 to 11 a different width, evenly decrease until you end up with 30 beads for this round.*

ROW 25: *Uses 24 beads and is a decrease row.* Brick stitch **4 beads, miss 1 bead**, repeat to end of the round.

ROW 26: *Uses 18 beads and is a decrease row.* **Brick stitch 3 beads, miss 1 bead**, repeat to end of round.

ROW 27: *Uses 12 beads and is a decrease row.* **Brick stitch 2 beads, miss 1 bead**, repeat to end of round.

ROW 28: *Uses 8 beads and is a decrease row.* **Brick stitch 2 beads, miss 1 bead**, repeat to end of the round.

The Basic Fish continued from page 58

WORKING THE MOUTH

Now you will need to change the angle of the beading so you can work 8 square stitches evenly around row 28, (see page 73 Changing Direction of Beads, for method).

ROW 29 CHANGING DIRECTION: Uses 8 cylinder beads (*this makes the mouth protrude*). *__We used Aqua DBR166.__*

Row 30: Square stitch 8 x 15/0 seed beads of a different colour on top of row 29. *__We used Pink 15/0' seed beads.__* Now run the thread through all the beads several times to make the mouth firm and sit in a round or oval shape. Weave thread ends securely into beading and cut.

WORKING THE FINS

THE DORSAL FIN - WORK 1: *__Use chart below__* The Dorsal Fin is positioned along the centre back spine line. Starting from the head end of the square stitched strip, square stitch the fin onto the spine line (centre back) of the fish. *Use cylinder beads.*

THE PECTORAL FIN - WORK 2, ONE ON EACH SIDE OF THE BODY: (*use chart below*) The Pectoral Fin is positioned on the lower front 8 rows down from the Dorsal Fin and four rows in from the Dorsal Fin. Work a second fin for the other side. *Use cylinder beads.*

THE EYE is a *Size 6/0 Seed Bead.* This is securely sewn onto the beading about six rows down from the edge of the fin. Using the same piece of thread string up approximately *13 x 11/0 Japanese Seed Beads or use 15 plus x 15/0 Japanese Seed Beads* and wrap these around the eye, securing in two places. *Repeat for other eye.*

MULTICOLOUR FISH KEY
Japanese Cylinder Beads 11/0

DELICA				QTY
DBR249	▲	▨	Purple	349
DBR245	▽	▨	Pink	280
DBR166	○	▨	Aqua	533
DBR41	■	▨	Silver	73
	⊗	○	Pink 15/0 Seed Bead	204

Also see other requirements on page 58.

Multicoloured Fish
worked from the basic pattern.

The multicoloured fish is worked from the basic pattern, using the charts below. We used pink, purple, aqua and green 11/0 cylinder beads. The centre strip was worked in square stitch as were the fins. The remainder of the fish was worked in brick stitch.

The eyes are 6/0 seed beads with one round of 20 x 15/0 Light Pink seed beads wrapped around this, then a second round of 12 x 15/0 Light Pink seed beads wrapped on top of the first round of seed beads.

The gills were three strands of 15 x Size 15/0 Light Pink seed beads hung on both sides of the fish.

Size 15/0 Light Pink seed beads were sewn onto the edges of the Dorsal Fin and Caudal Fin after the fish was complete.

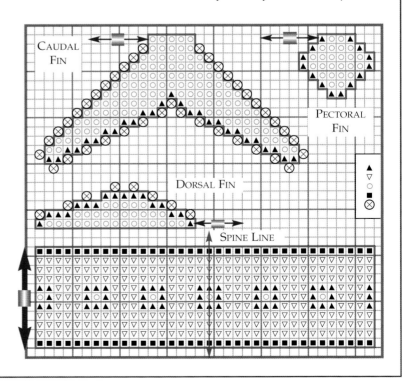

Blue Beaded Fish BY JILL OXTON

The body of the blue fish is worked using brick stitch around a glass marble. The fins were worked in square stitch, directly onto the beaded body and the eyes and gills are seed bead embellishments.

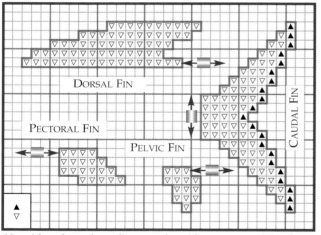

Use either chart, depending on what side you are working from.

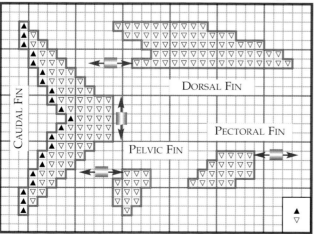

STITCHES USED
SQUARE STITCH SEE PAGE 70
BRICK STITCH SEE PAGE 66

JAPANESE CYLINDER BEADS 11/0 KEY QTY

DELICA				
DBR243	▲		Medium Blue	767
DBR257	▽		Light Blue	201

YOU WILL ALSO NEED:
2 x 6/0 Dark Blue Seed Beads *(for the eyes)*
70 x 15/0 Light Blue Japanese Seed Beads *(eyes & gills)*
Blue Nymo D Thread
No. 10 Blunt Beading Needle
1 x Clear Glass marble 21mm diameter
2 x Thin Silver Foil Chocolate Wrappers

Depending on the size of the marble used, you may have to pad the marble with metallic foil or adjust the width of the strip for rows 1 to 11. We used a glass marble 21mm in diameter (see diagram on page 53).

THE BODY (All Medium Blue except for row 1)

ROW 1: Work ladder stitch 36 beads wide using *11 Medium Blue, 1 Light Blue*, repeat twice until strip is 36 beads wide. *This should be wide enough to fit around the marble when joined, adjust if necessary.*

The light blue beads indicate the position for attaching the fins. There are three fins at the front which are distributed evenly around the body.

ROWS 2 TO 11: Brick stitch 10 more rows using Medium Blue beads. Join the short edges of the strip together and place over the marble.

ROW 12: *Uses 30 beads and is a decrease row. *Brick stitch 5 miss 1*, repeat to the end of the round. If you have worked rows 1 to 11 a different width, evenly decrease until you end up with 30 beads for this round.*

ROW 13: *Uses 30 beads. Work brick stitch all around.*

ROW 14: *Uses 30 beads. Work brick stitch all around.*

ROW 15: *Uses 24 beads and is a decrease row. *Brick stitch 4, miss 1*, repeat to end of the round.*

ROW 16: *Uses 24 beads. Work brick stitch all around.*

ROW 17: *Uses 20 beads and is a decrease row. *Brick stitch 5, miss 1*, repeat to end of the round.*

continued on page 61

Row 18: *Uses 20 beads.* Work brick stitch all around.

Row 19: *Uses 16 beads and is a decrease row.* *Brick stitch 4, miss 1*, repeat to end of the round.

Row 20: *Uses 16 beads.* Work brick stitch all around.

Row 21: *Uses 12 beads and is a decrease row.* *Brick stitch 3, miss 1*, repeat to end of the round.

Row 22: *Uses 12 beads.* Work brick stitch all around.

CONSTRUCTING THE TAIL: *See chart on page 60.*
The tail is worked in square stitch on the end of row 22. Pinch the tail end so it folds in half vertically and change the angle of the beading so you can work five square stitch centred along one edge *(see page 73 Changing Direction of Beads, for method)*. This is the first row of the Caudal Fin chart above.

Note: One of the light blue beads from Row 1 should indicate the centre of the back (the spine line). This should line up with the vertical edge of the tail.

When the tail has been worked, weave thread back down to the base of tail and join the brick stitch beads on the other side of the body to the square stitched tail to close up the small hole and finish off by weaving in thread ends securely.

Remove the marble from the beading and pack the tail end of the beading with one or two of the foil wrappers, insert marble and pinch tail into shape.

CONSTRUCTING THE HEAD:
You should now be on the other end of body next to the first row worked and using **11/0 Medium Blue**.

Row 23: *Uses 30 beads and is a decrease row.* *Brick stitch 5 miss 1*, repeat to the end of the round. *If you have worked rows 1 to 11 a different width, evenly decrease until you end up with 30 beads for this round.*

Row 24: *Uses 24 beads and is a decrease row.* *Brick stitch 4, miss 1*, repeat to end of the round.

Row 25: *Uses 18 beads and is a decrease row.* *Brick stitch 3, miss 1*, repeat to end of the round.

Row 26: *Uses 16 beads and is a decrease row.* *Brick stitch 8, miss 1*, repeat to end of the round.

Row 27: *Uses 12 beads and is a decrease row.* *Brick stitch 3, miss 1*, repeat to end of the round.

WORKING THE MOUTH
Now you will need to change the angle of the beading so you can work 8 square stitches evenly around row 28, (see page 73 Changing Direction for method).

Row 28 CHANGING DIRECTION: *Uses 8 x* **11/0 Medium Blue** *beads and is a decrease row.* *Work 2, miss 1*, repeat to end of the round.

Now run the thread through all the beads several times to make the mouth a round shape.

Row 29 SQUARE STITCH: *Uses 8 x* **11/0 Light Blue** *beads.* Work square stitch all around on top of row 28.

Run the thread through all of the beads several times so the mouth sits in a round or oval shape, then weave thread into beading to secure and finish off.

WORKING THE FINS

THE DORSAL FIN - WORK 1: *(Use chart on page 60).* The Dorsal Fin is positioned along the centre back. Starting from the light blue bead at the front of the body *(which indicates the spine line)* square stitch the fin onto the spine line (centre back) of the fish.

THE PECTORAL FIN - WORK 2, ONE ON EACH SIDE OF THE BODY: *(Use chart on page 60).* The Pectoral Fin is positioned on the lower front. Starting from the light blue bead on the side of the body, square stitch the fin horizontally on the side. Work a second fin for the other side.

THE PELVIC FIN - WORK 2, ONE ON EACH SIDE OF THE BODY: *(Use chart on page 60).* The Pelvic Fin is positioned horizontally at the tail end of the fish, about 7 or 8 rows down from the Dorsal Fin, and lining up vertically on the fish in a similar position to that on the chart. Work a second pelvic fin on the other side.

THE EYE is a **6/0 Dark Blue Seed Bead**. This was securely sewn onto the beading about six rows down from the edge of the fin. Using the same piece of thread we then strung up approximately 15 x **15/0 Light Blue Japanese Seed Beads** and wrapped these around the eye, securing in two places. *Repeat for the other eye.*

THE GILLS are one strand of 18 x **15/0 Light Blue Japanese Seed Beads** draped behind and below the eye. *Repeat for the other side.*

Pink Beaded Fish BY JILL OXTON

The Pink Fish is a variation of the Blue Fish on page 60. The centre section of the body of the pink fish is worked in a strip using square stitch, which is then joined into a round and placed around a glass marble. We used both Japanese Cylinder Beads and Japanese Seed Beads in the fish.

Using this method I found it easier to incorporate a pattern/texture on the centre strip. We used a mixture of size 11/0 Delica's and Japanese Seed Beads for this.

The head and tail end were worked using brick stitch. The fins were worked in square stitch, directly onto the beaded body and the eyes and gills are seed bead embellishments.

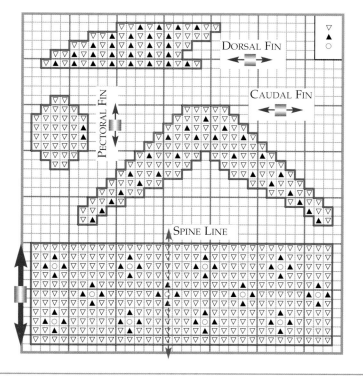

STITCHES USED

SQUARE STITCH SEE PAGE 70
BRICK STITCH SEE PAGE 66

JAPANESE CYLINDER BEADS 11/0 KEY			QTY
DELICA			
DBR624	▽	☐ Light Pink	805
JAPANESE SEED BEADS 11/0			
	▲	☐ Light Pink	167
	○	☐ Light Blue	12

YOU WILL ALSO NEED:

2 x 6/0 Dark Pink Seed Beads for the eyes
34 x 11/0 Medium Pink Japanese Seed Beads
Beige or Silver Nymo D Thread
No. 10 Blunt Beading Needle
1 x Clear Glass marble
2 x Thin Silver Foil Chocolate Wrappers

Depending on the size of the marble used, you may have to adjust this pattern. We used a light green glass marble, the sort used for filling vases for floral displays.

THE BODY (*Light Pink Cylinder & Seed Beads*)

ROWS 1 TO 11: Work a strip in square stitch following the chart (bottom left) **32 beads wide x 11 beads high**. *This should be wide enough to fit around the marble when joined, adjust if necessary.*

Join the short edges of the strip together and place over the marble, this should be a snug fit.

ROW 12: *Uses 30 beads and is a decrease row.* Brick stitch ***4 cylinder and 1 seed bead three times then miss 1 bead***, repeat once more.

If you have worked rows 1 to 11 a different width, evenly decrease until you end up with 30 beads for this round.

ROW 13: *Uses 30 beads.* Brick stitch ***4 cylinder and 1 seed bead***, repeat all around, positioning the seed bead between those on the previous row.

ROW 14: *Uses 30 beads.* Same as row 13.

ROW 15: *Uses 24 beads and is a decrease row.* Brick stitch ***4 cylinder beads, miss 1 bead***, repeat to end of the round.

ROW 16: *Uses 24 beads.* Brick stitch ***3 cylinder and 1 seed bead***, repeat to end of round.

ROW 17: *Uses 20 beads and is a decrease row.* Brick stitch ***5 cylinder beads, miss 1 bead***, repeat to end of the round.

continued on page 63

ROW 18: *Uses 20 beads.* Brick stitch ***4 cylinder and 1 seed bead***, repeat to end of round.

ROW 19: *Uses 16 beads and is a decrease row.* Brick stitch ***4 cylinder beads, miss 1***, repeat to end of round.

ROW 20: *Uses 16 beads.* Brick stitch ***3 cylinder and 1 seed bead***, repeat to end of round.

ROW 21: *Uses 12 beads and is a decrease row.* *Brick stitch ***3 cylinder beads, miss 1 bead***, repeat to end of round.

ROW 22: *Uses 12 beads.* Brick stitch ***2 cylinder and 1 seed bead***, repeat to end of round.

ROW 23: *Uses 8 beads and is a decrease row.* *Brick stitch ***2 cylinder beads, miss 1 bead***, repeat to end of round.

CONSTRUCTING THE TAIL: *See chart on page 62.*

The tail is worked in square stitch on the end of row 23. Pinch the tail end so it folds in half horizontally and change the angle of the beading so you can work five square stitch centred along the top edge *(see page 73 Changing Direction for method)*. This is the first row of the Caudal Fin chart.

Note: The centre of the tail should line up with the spine line of the fish. See chart marking on square stitched strip.

Weave thread ends in and finish off tail by weaving in thread securely.

Remove the marble from the beading and pack the tail end of the beading with one or two of the foil wrappers, insert marble and pinch the back of the body into a pleasing shape.

CONSTRUCTING THE HEAD:

You should now be on the other end of body next to the first row worked.

ROW 24: *Uses 30 beads and is a decrease row.* Brick stitch ***4 cylinder and 1 seed bead three times then miss 1 bead***, repeat once more.

If you have worked rows 1 to 11 a different width, evenly decrease until you end up with 30 beads for this round.

ROW 25: *Uses 24 beads and is a decrease row.* Brick stitch ***3 cylinder beads, miss 1 bead***, repeat to end of round.

ROW 26: *Uses 18 beads and is a decrease row.* Brick stitch ***1 cylinder, 1 seed, 1 cylinder bead, miss 1 bead***, repeat to end of round.

ROW 27: *Uses 12 beads and is a decrease row.* Brick stitch ***2 cylinder beads, miss 1 bead***, repeat to end of round.

ROW 28: *Uses 8 beads and is a decrease row.* Brick stitch ***1 cylinder, 1 seed, miss 1 bead***, repeat to end of the round.

WORKING THE MOUTH ROW 29:

Now you will need to change the angle of the beading so you can work 8 square stitches evenly around row 28, *(see page 73 Changing Direction for method).*

ROW 29 CHANGING DIRECTION: *Uses 8 beads and is a decrease row.* Using *__Medium Pink Seed Beads__*, ***Work 2 seed beads, miss 1 bead***, repeat to end of the round.

Now run the thread through all the beads several times to make the mouth firm and sit correctly. Weave thread ends into beading to secure.

WORKING THE FINS

THE DORSAL FIN - WORK 1: *(see chart on page 62)* The Dorsal Fin is positioned along the centre back spine line. Starting from the head end of the square stitched strip, square stitch the fin onto the spine line (centre back) of the fish. *Use cylinder beads.*

THE PECTORAL FIN - WORK 2, ONE ON EACH SIDE OF THE BODY: *(see chart on page 62)* The Pectoral Fin is positioned on the lower front, 8 rows down from the Dorsal Fin and four rows in from the front edge of the Dorsal Fin. Work a second fin for the other side. *Use cylinder beads.*

THE EYE is a *__6/0 Dark Pink Seed Bead__*. This was securely sewn onto the beading about six rows down from the edge of the fin. Using the same piece of thread we then strung up approximately *13 x __Medium Pink Seed Beads__* and wrapped these around the eye, securing in two places. We then strung up *10 x __Light Pink Seed Beads__* and wrapped these around the eye above the medium pink seed beads, securing in two places.

The Purple and Green Fish was worked using the Basic Beaded Fish instructions on page 58, but we did not work the pattern on this strip, instead we alternated 11/0 Delica DBR135 Purple and 11/0 Japanese seed beads, carrying this through to the rest of the body.

To do this we worked one Delica DBR135, then one bead picked up at random from a mixture of Mill Hill Antique Glass Beads consisting of 03034 Royal Amethyst; 03053 Purple Passion; 03020 Dusty Mauve and 03035 Royal Green, but any combination of colours can be used.

The fins were from the Pink Fish on page 62, and were worked using 11/0 Delica's DBR27 Green and DBR135 Purple.

The main part of the fins were worked using green and the outside edges used purple. Each eye was wrapped with 12 x Mill Hill Antique Glass Beads in 03035 Royal Green.

Using a mixture of 11/0 Delica's and 11/0 Seed Beads did cause the body to be larger and a little shapeless compared to the other fish, so when it was complete the section between the dorsal fin and the caudal fin was sculpted by stitching through the beads on both sides and flattening it a little along and below the spine. See broken line on picture indicating the sculpted section (stitching line).

The fish was stuck onto the shell using E6000 glue.

Fishing Rod *(10 cm (4") high)*

YOU WILL NEED

36cm (14") x 24 gauge wire.

36cm (14") x 26 gauge wire.

6" of fine silver chain.

1 half used roll of Nymo thread.

14 x DBL41 size 8/0 Delica's

1 Shepherd Hook

1 x 3mm jump ring

1cm Sadi Metallic Thread
   (for the worm - optional)

The fishing rod is 10cm (4") high and was made by bending a 36cm (14") length of 24 gauge wire in half and twisting it for two thirds of it's length, leaving a small loop at the top (see Diag. 1).

14 x DBL41 were threaded onto the end of the wire. *(The ends of the wire were wrapped to form a base which was flattened, bent at a 90° angle to the rod and used to glue the rod to the shell.*

DIAG. 1

26 gauge wire was wrapped around the wire below and directly above the beads. It was also used to secure the half used roll of Nymo thread to the rod and the end of the 15cm (6") length of silver chain. This was then twisted several times to tighten up the wrap and the ends of the wire formed into a round handle.

The chain was secured to the centre of the rod section using 26 gauge wire threaded through the loop. A jump ring and shepherd's hook was attached to the end. The end of the hook was trimmed a little and the *worm* attached.

The Stitches

Other Information

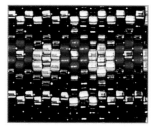

BRICK STITCH

FRINGES

SQUARE STITCH

RIGHT ANGLE WEAVE

SPIRAL ROPE STITCH

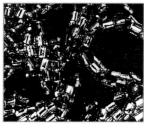

PETERBURG CHAIN

LADDER STITCH

Use this stitch to make straps or as a foundation for brick stitch. Our diagram doesn't show it, but you can stitch through each bead twice to strengthen the ladder. Keep tension firm, but not tight or you will find it difficult to catch up the thread when working the second row.

SLIP KNOT

DIAG. 1

DIAG. 2

1. Make a loop with the tail end on top. (Diag 1).

2. Pull a loop from the tail end through the loop. (Diag 2).

3. Holding both ends of thread, draw the loop up, tightening the knot.

4. Pull the tail end a little, to check the slip knot will close.

BRICK STITCH

Diagram 1 (below): The top row shows the foundation row of ladder stitch. The second row is brick stitch. **At the beginning of every row always pick up two beads**. Pass the needle behind and then over the loop and back down through the bead the thread is exiting, so that the bead is hanging on a thread loop. Continue by picking up one bead at a time, making one stitch per loop and pulling thread taut. *brick stitch can be worked from right to left, or left to right.*

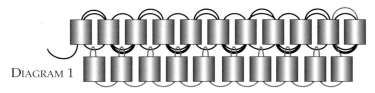

DIAGRAM 1

BRICK STITCH INCREASE ON THE OUTSIDE EDGE

Work ladder stitch to desired length (Diagram 2).

Ladder stitch can be worked from left to right, or right to left.

DIAGRAM 2

BRICK STITCH DECREASE ON THE OUTSIDE EDGE

Weave thread back through beads to the correct position and commence the row with two beads (Diagram3).

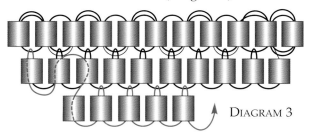

DIAGRAM 3

STARTING & FINISHING THREADS IN BRICK STITCH

Weave thread ends in and out of at least five beads and then diagonally through another five beads. Pull taut and cut thread.
To start a thread, take thread through about five beads, pull end into bead and then weave in and out of at least five beads to sewing position.

ATTACHING A FRINGE TO BRICK STITCH

Exit from bead and pick up required number of fringe beads. Run thread back through all the beads, except the last. Weave over to the next bead and repeat.

The fringing diagram (below) shows four different ways of attaching a fringe. You can also use these methods on the surface of the beading as well as on the edge.

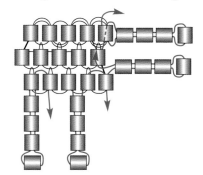

TUBULAR CONCENTRIC BRICK STITCH

Join the end beads of the ladder together with the thread coming out of the bottom of the bead, pick up two beads and make your first stitch. End the row by joining the last bead to the first bead and coming out of the bottom of the last bead. Pick up two beads to commence following rows.

TUBULAR SPIRAL BRICK STITCH

Make a ladder, pick up one bead and make your first stitch. At the end of the row, attach one bead to the loop of the first bead of that row and you will start spiralling.

FLAT BRICK STITCH

(also known as Comanche Weave)

The top row (beads 1-8) of the diagram, below is ladder stitch. This is the foundation row for brick stitch. Work each stitch twice, *but not tightly,* before adding a new bead. *This strengthens the foundation and also helps it to sit better.*

Beads 9-16 show the first row of brick stitch. *Brick Stitch can be worked with one, two, or more beads. See double drop, beads 41-46.*

Start by picking up two beads. Pass the needle behind and then over the loop and back down through the bead the thread is exiting, so the bead is hanging on a thread loop (beads 9-10). Continue by picking up one bead at a time, making one stitch per loop and tightening thread to position beads correctly.

When starting a row always add two beads if working a single drop (see beads 9-10; 17-18; 25-26; 33-34), four beads if working a double drop (beads 41-44), six beads for a triple drop, and so on.

When you reach the end of the row, pick up two beads and work back the other way (beads 17-18).

Decrease within a piece by not stitching in a loop (beads 30-31).

Increase within a piece by stitching two beads within a loop (beads 27-28).

CIRCULAR CONCENTRIC BRICK STITCH

(from the inside out)

Keep your tension even and firm but work the first two rounds with a looser tension. *We have started our round with three beads but the number of beads on the first circle is flexible, depending on the pattern. The number of beads added to subsequent rows are determined by the size of the bead. Increase enough to form a flat solid surface.*

1. Cut your thread around 1 metre (40") long and make a slip knot with the tail end. Make sure that the tail slides through the knot (see slip knot diagram on page 66).

2. Round 1: Pick up two beads to begin the round. Pass the needle through the slip knot from the bottom to the top and back through bead 2. (See Diagram 1.)

3. Pick up one bead (3) and pass the needle through the slip knot and back through the bead.

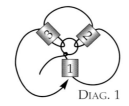

DIAG. 1

4. *Take the needle and thread back through bead 1 and out through bead 3* (Diagram 2). Close up the slip knot by pulling the tail thread.

This attaches the first bead to the last bead of the round, and also makes the first bead of the round (1) sit properly. This is done at the end of every round.

5. Round 2: (see Diagram 2) is an Increase Round. Pick up two beads (4 and 5). Pass the needle through the loop between beads 3 and 1 and back through bead 5.

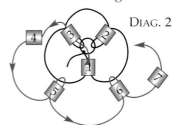

DIAG. 2

6. *Pick up one bead and pass the needle through the next loop* (between beads 1 and 2).

7. Increase by stitching a second bead (7) to the same loop.

8. Repeat from * to * for the loop between beads 2 and 3 and work another increase. There should now be six beads in the second round.

9. Attach the last bead of this round to the first bead (4) by working a brick stitch through it. *Every time you begin a round you will need to pick up two beads.*

10. Continue in this manner, increasing and decreasing as indicated on the pattern.

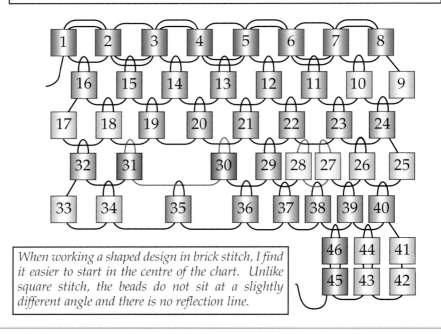

When working a shaped design in brick stitch, I find it easier to start in the centre of the chart. Unlike square stitch, the beads do not sit at a slightly different angle and there is no reflection line.

Our diagrams show one bead per side, but you can use two or more. *Two beads per side were used for the Cherry Amulet.*

Right angle weave or RAW, is worked clockwise and anti-clockwise. If your previous circle was worked clockwise then your next circle will be worked anti-clockwise and vice versa. Our instructions reflect the direction of our diagrams.

FIRST ROW/ MAKING A CHAIN

1 Leaving a tail of 15cm (6″) for weaving in later, string up four beads. Run the thread through the first three beads again to form a circle. Pull the thread taut so the beads are touching.

2 Pick up three beads on your needle and working anti-clockwise, bring the needle and thread back though the last vertical bead (called the connecting bead) and the first two beads just added. You should now have two squares.

3 Add three more beads. Working clockwise, take the needle and thread through the connecting bead in the previous square (the last bead you came through in the previous square) and the first two beads just added. You should now have three squares.

Alternate steps 2 and 3 until your chain is the desired length.

SECOND & SUBSEQUENT ROWS

4 Add three beads. Working anticlockwise, pass the needle through the last horizontal bead of the previous row.

5 Add two beads. Working clockwise, pass the needle through the horizontal bead of the previous row and the last vertical bead of the previous square. Continue working in this manner to the end of the row.

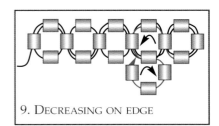

1

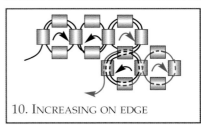

2

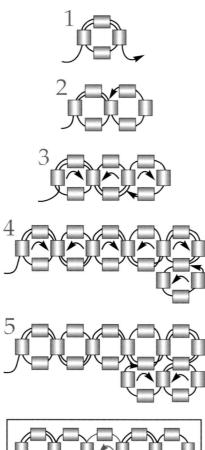

3

4

5

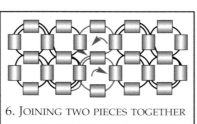

6. JOINING TWO PIECES TOGETHER

9. DECREASING ON EDGE

10. INCREASING ON EDGE

7. DECREASING WITHIN

8. INCREASING WITHIN

FILLING IN OR EMBELLISHING RAW

When all RAW is complete, it can be filled in or embellished using the same or a contrasting bead (*the green bead in our diagram*). Use one strand of Nymo D when working the RAW and filling in, as this extra step can cause thread build up. *Work from left to right, or right to left.*

RAW BAG FROM CS&B ISSUE 48

Amulet Bag worked in RAW using 2 beads per side and filled in with the same colour bead.

FROM SQUARE STITCH TO RIGHT ANGLE WEAVE - see page 75

Pictured above is a spiral rope chain bracelet using 11/0 Delica's DBR35 and DBR6 and earrings which are a variation on spiral rope chain using bugle beads the length of four DBR's.

Step 1 - Pick up five core beads and one bugle for outside row.

Step 2 - same as instructions.

Step 3 - Pick up one core bead, one bugle and pass needle through the last four core beads added in Step 1.

Steps 4, 5 & 6 - same as instructions.

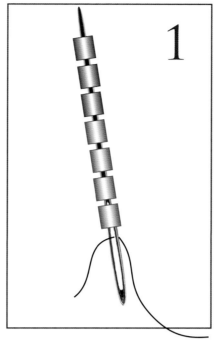

STEP 1: Pick up four core beads and three main colour (outside) beads. Draw them down to the end of your thread, leaving a tail of about 10cm (4") to be woven in later.

The thread tail is now the bottom of the chain and the working end is the top.

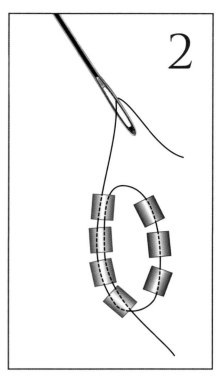

STEP 2: Pass your needle back through the four core beads, from the bottom to the top and pull the thread to form an irregular loop.

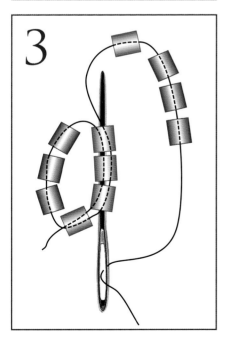

STEP 3: Pick up one core bead and three outside beads. Pass your needle through the last three core beads added in Step 1.

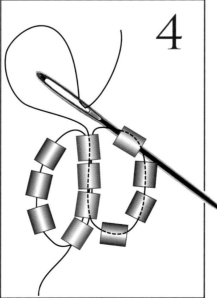

STEP 4: Pass your needle through the single core bead added in Step 3 and pull thread firmly. *The core bead should now be sitting on top of the other core beads.*

STEP 5: Adjust the outside beads just added so they are sitting snugly next to the previous outside row.

STEP 6: Repeat Steps 3, 4 & 5 until your chain is the desired length.

It will take a few repetitions before spiral rope stitch becomes evident, but each new row of outside (blue) beads should be one bead higher than the previous row.

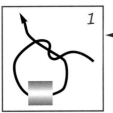

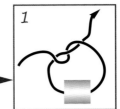

The diagrams on the left are for the left handed.

The diagrams on the right are for the right handed.

Square stitch in DBR 11/0's at actual size.

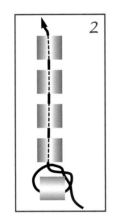

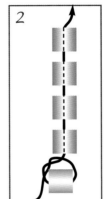

TO START: Cut your thread as long as you can manage it and thread your needle.

DIAGRAM 1: Tie a stopper bead onto the tail end of the thread. Don't knot, as this bead will be removed later. It's purpose is to stop your beads falling off the thread. Leave a tail of at least 10cm (4"). This will be woven in later.

Square stitch in DBR 11/0's at 150%.

THE FIRST ROW

DIAGRAM 2: String up the first row of beads, from the bottom to the top, following the pattern.

SECOND ROW

DIAGRAM 3: (*Right- handers work clockwise, left-handers work anti clockwise*).

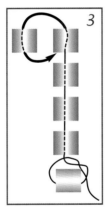

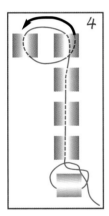

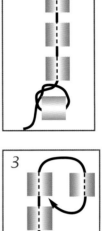

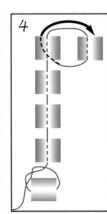

The second row will be your hardest row as you are attaching beads to beads that have been strung up and which can slide about. Use your stopper bead to adjust the tension when working this row.

Following the colours in the pattern, pick up one bead, leaving it on your needle. Pass the needle from the bottom to the top of the last bead and then back down from the top to the bottom of the new bead **DIAGRAM 4.**

DIAGRAM 5 *Pick up a bead and attach it to the bead in the previous column adjacent to it, passing the needle from the bottom to the top of the bead and then the top to bottom of the new bead*. Repeat this step to finish row.

DIAGRAM 6 shows the second row finished.

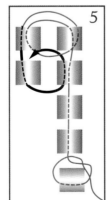

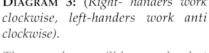

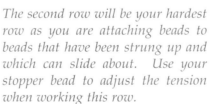

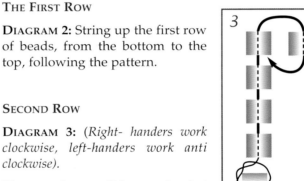

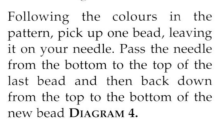

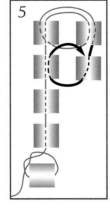

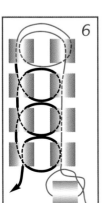

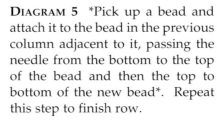

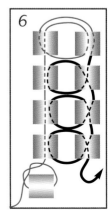

See page 71 for third row.

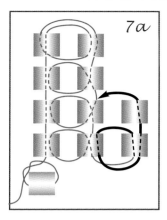

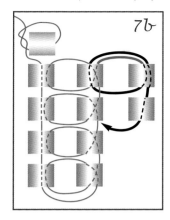

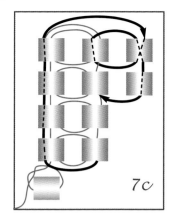

DIAGRAM 7A - WORKING THE THIRD ROW IN REVERSE.

Pro's & Cons..............

It is much easier to follow the chart as you don't have to turn your work.

The beading is stretchy and drapey, suitable for pictures, amulet bags, clothing and fitting *and or* stretching over items.

I couldn't get a perfect tension, and my work distorted. My tension was different working square stitch from the bottom to the top than it was working from the top to the bottom, which caused the distortion. I now use either method 7b or 7c when working square stitch for a perfectly flat square piece. BUT just because I couldn't manage it, this method may work for you!

See notes on page 73 about my first attempt at square stitch using this method.

DIAGRAM 7B - TURN YOUR WORK SO YOU ARE ALWAYS WORKING FROM THE TOP DOWN.

Pro's & Cons..............

I could achieve a perfect tension.

Beading is stretchy and drapey, suitable for pictures, amulet bags, clothing and fitting over items.

Easy for symmetrical designs, (one half of the pattern is a mirror image).

Harder to read chart. As every second row is upside down, you have to read the chart from the bottom up while working from the top down. To do this I tie a piece of coloured thread onto the 'back' of the beading and mark every second column of the chart with a small dot to correspond, so that I remember when working these columns to read the chart from the bottom up.

Great for stretching your mind!

DIAGRAM 7C - RUN THE THREAD BACK UP THROUGH THE PREVIOUS ROW AND WORK FROM THE TOP DOWN.

Pro's & Cons..............

This is one of the stronger methods.

It is easy to follow your chart.

Ideal for narrow firm/rigid pieces such as belts and bracelets.

There <u>will</u> be distortion or buckling with larger pieces if you don't pull the thread back up through the previous row at exactly the same tension every time.

More thread build up inside the beads.

Thread shows along the outside edge.

This can distort a design by tighening up the columns, not the rows.

7D You can also run the thread through the previous row and back down through row just worked. This causes more thread build up but the thread along the edge is less obvious.

THE GREEN COLOURED DIAGRAMS BELOW ARE FOR THE LEFT HANDED.

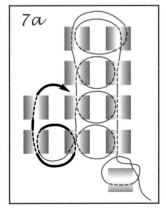

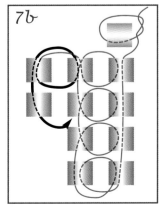

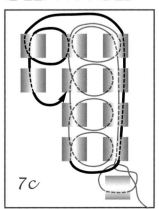

ATTACHING FRINGES

There are several different ways to attach fringes to your beading.

Add them between the beads (Diagram 1), aligned to the beads (Diagram 2), and through the bead (Diagram 3).

In all cases you need a bead *(or beads - see Three Bead Picot)* at the base which the thread only goes into once, to hold the fringe beads on the thread.

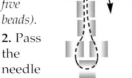

Diag. 1

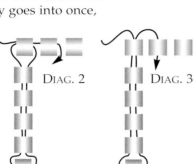

Diag. 2   Diag. 3

THREE BEAD PICOT

1. Bring your needle out of the bead at the bottom and string up at least four beads.

(Our diagram shows five beads).

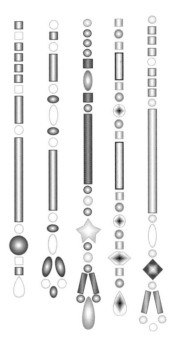

2. Pass the needle and thread back up through the first two beads strung and then through the next bead on the edge of the beaded item. You have now completed one fringe.

3. Bring the needle through the second bead and continue as above until the fringe is complete.

FRINGE IDEAS
BY MARY MOTT

JOINING TWO PIECES OF BEADING TOGETHER

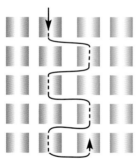

I find it easier to join the seams of square stitch beading together using a simplified version of square stitch rather than trying to catch up the thread on the outside edge of the beading. This method is also stronger.

When joining two pieces of beading together, take care that you do not pull the thread too tightly or the seam will not fold properly. After every few stitches I fold the item into its intended position to check my joining tension.

When the seam has been joined together, I work a return journey in the opposite direction for added strength.

Weave all thread ends into the beading, see below.

STARTING & FINISHING THREADS

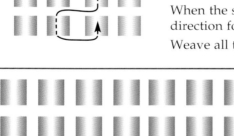

Start of new thread
End of old thread

The red line on the diagram indicates finishing off the thread and the black line indicates starting a new thread in square stitch.

You will need to weave in and out of at least five beads to secure the thread and stop it slipping *(more with finer thread).*

Avoid starting and finishing on the edges, as this is where the thread builds up quickest and may cause a problem when joining two pieces of beading together.

For the first weave when starting a thread, and the last weave when finishing a thread, I like to run the thread though at least ten beads, but preferably a distance of 5cm (2"), depending on the piece, before cutting the thread as sometimes the movement of the beading, (for example when wearing an amulet bag) can on occasion, cause an end of thread to poke out. By ending with a long length of thread run through the beads, you have two options; 1 - Cut the end off, which is a bit risky; 2 - Unpick a little more of the end, thread it onto a needle and weave it back in.

Above is my first attempt at square stitch, the result of which I found very unsatisfactory. There was a problem with my tension when working square stitch up and down as shown in diagram 7a and no amount of wishing or pulling would bring it back into shape.

I started adapting the stitch and found that I got a near perfect tension by turning the work after every row and always working from the top down. (See A on the photograph above). I now read the chart in columns, (not rows) and hold the piece sideways in my hand while working, using methods 7b or 7c shown on page 66.

It is a good idea to work a test piece to check your tension and decide on the method you wish to use. If you change your method after starting the piece, it does show as you can see from the top of this beading.

The bracelets are an ideal item to learn square stitch with. I would suggest you only start a large piece when you are happy and relaxed with your tension and working square stitch. It doesn't take long! And, you will save yourself some heartache.

CHANGING THE DIRECTION OF BEADS

I use this method if I want to form a round using square stitch or am working around a form and wish to work a base (as for the needlecase on page 50) as I find it easier and more accurate to work a base for a round by working from the outside edge into the centre, rather than from the centre to the outside edge.

Changing direction of the beads was also used when working the square stitch fins onto the brick stitch sections of the Beaded Fish on pages 53 to 60.

TO START: Work a strip in square stitch and make into a round by joining both ends together using square stitch.

Try to make the number of columns in a strip divisible by 4, 5 or 6 as you will invariable have to decrease at some stage and decreasing distributed evenly on a round looks much nicer than irregular decreases and will also form a pattern.

DIAGRAM 1: CHANGING THE DIRECTION OF THE BEADS

DIAG. 1

Coming out of the centre of a bead on one edge of the round or beading, pick up 1 bead and go back through the bead you just came out of, now go up through the next bead. Repeat all around.

When you stitch the next row on top of this row, it will straighten up the beads in this row.

The blue beads on the diagram indicate the square stitched strip. The pink beads indicate the first round of changing direction.

DIAGRAM 2: CHANGING THE DIRECTION OF BEADS AND DECREASING AT THE SAME TIME
*Diagram 2 illustrates decreasing on every fifth bead ie *work 4 miss 1*.*

DIAG. 2

Coming out of the centre of a bead on one edge of the round or beading, pick up 1 bead and go back through the bead you just came out of, then go up through the next bead. Work 3 more stitches in this manner, miss 1 bead, work 4, miss 1, all around.

DIAGRAM 3 TO TIGHTEN AND STRAIGHTEN THE BEADS:
Run thread through all the beads of this row twice and pull taut.

DIAG. 3

Changing the direction of beads was used in the locket pictured left, from Cross Stitch and Beading Issue 56.

INCREASING AND DECREASING

When working shaped designs in square stitch, it is easier to decrease than increase. To do this you need to start at the widest or highest row of the design. The trade off is that you will have a reflection when working the other half as the angle of the bead changes.

You can work square stitch from the top of the design down to the bottom, increasing and decreasing as required by using the methods illustrated, or working one or two rows and then weaving back to increase on a firm base. There are different variations on these and practice makes perfect, but it will not take long before increasing and decreasing become automatic.

Be careful of thread buildup in beads if you weave back and forth a lot.

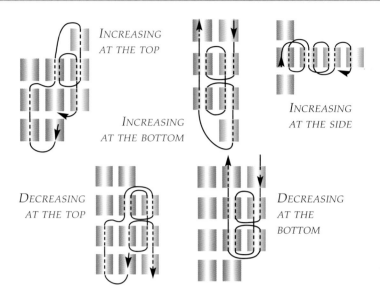

INCREASING AT THE TOP

INCREASING AT THE SIDE

INCREASING AT THE BOTTOM

DECREASING AT THE TOP

DECREASING AT THE BOTTOM

REFLECTIONS

Top: Voluptuous Mermaids from CS&B Issue 51.
Bottom: Red Geisha from CS&B Issue 52.

When I first started working in square stitch I found it easier to decrease rather than increase, so I used to start in the widest part, work one half of the design and then turn the work and work the other half. Unfortunately with this method sometimes the results are unsatisfactory as you do get a reflection change in the beads as they lie in a different direction. The mermaid is a perfect example.

For the Geisha we started at the bottom of the design and had to add the bottom of the sleeve last, hence the reflection where the sleeve separates from the body as once again the beads lie in a different direction.

THREAD PATH FOR WORKING A SHAPED EDGE

A double stitch is worked here so both beads sit properly. Although not always shown on this diagram, I do this for all increases except single beads.

It is unavoidable, but if adding only one bead, the thread will show.

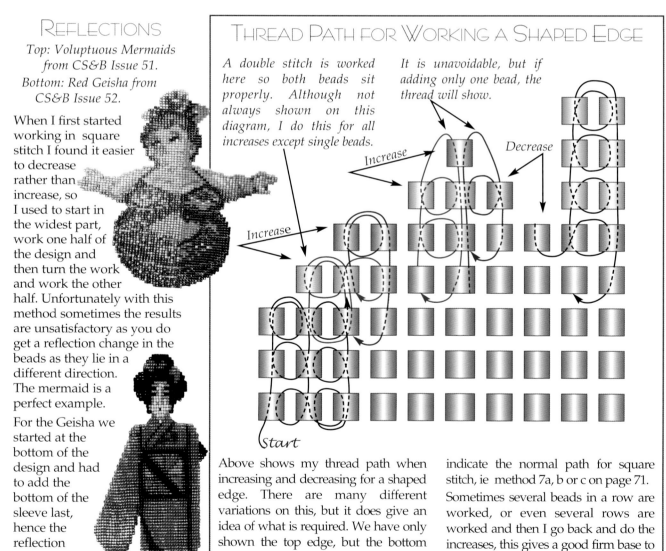

Increase

Decrease

Increase

Start

Above shows my thread path when increasing and decreasing for a shaped edge. There are many different variations on this, but it does give an idea of what is required. We have only shown the top edge, but the bottom edge is worked in a similar manner.

Pink and green beads with pink and green lines indicate the weaving pattern for increasing/decreasing. Blue beads indicate the normal path for square stitch, ie method 7a, b or c on page 71.

Sometimes several beads in a row are worked, or even several rows are worked and then I go back and do the increases, this gives a good firm base to attach the beads to (see the first three columns of beads on the left).

Decreasing is much easier as you just weave back to the correct position.

COMBINING STITCHES

SQUARE STITCH TO BRICK STITCH

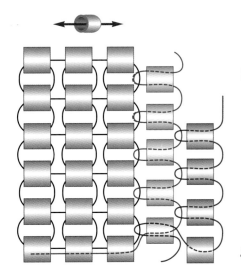

The blue beads on the diagram indicate square stitch.

Brick stitch is indicated by, 1st row pink beads, 2nd row green beads.

We used this method for the pots on pages 26 to 28, working from the outside edge into the centre in brick stitch.

The square stitch was worked first and then the brick stitch. Worked over a form (*a cardboard shape the required size*), this was an easy way to ensure the base was the correct size for the pot.

At the beginning of each round or row in brick stitch, add two beads on the first stitch, then add one bead at a time.

When working 'in the round', complete the round by taking the last stitch of the round into the first bead of the round to make it sit correctly (*blue thread on diagram*). Then bring the thread down to the bottom of the bead to start the next row, again starting with two beads (*green thread on diagram*).

SQUARE STITCH TO RIGHT ANGLE WEAVE (RAW)

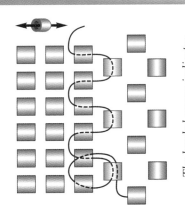

The beaded arrow indicates direction of the hole in the bead.

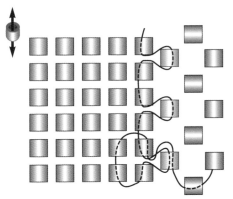

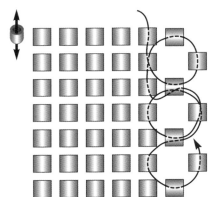

DIAGRAM 1

Working RAW on the side of square stitch.

DIAGRAM 2

Working RAW on the top of square stitch.

DIAGRAM 3 (VARIATION)

I quite often use this method for edgings on amulet bags.

BRICK STITCH OR PEYOTE STITCH TO SQUARE STITCH

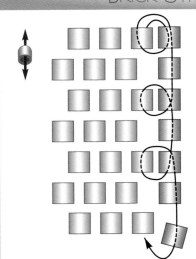

Diagram Left: Coming out of the brick or peyote stitch, square stitch one bead to the first brick or peyote stitch bead, add a bead, square stitch the next bead to brick or peyote stitch, add a bead. Continue to end of the row. This method does leave little holes in the work, but they can be quite decorative.

This method can be worked for beading in the round as we did for the Rosebud Needlecase featured in CS&B Issue No. 46 (pictured on the right) using an even number of rows. It can also be used for attaching square stitch to flat brick or peyote stitch using an uneven count/number of beads.

BEAD TIPS

also known as fold over cover tips, bead tips, clam shell tips or Charlotte crimps.

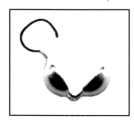

The bead tip acts as a transition between the beading thread and metal findings. Using it, rather than stitching your finding onto beaded jewellery, will finish the piece off and make it look more professional.

To Attach A Bead Tip

(See the diagrams on the right.)

Pass the thread through the bead tip (there is a hole at the base), run it through at least two rows of the beading if possible and then bring the thread back out through the hole in the cover tip. Thread a bead onto one of the threads (this stops the knot from falling through the hole) and tie two or three knots. Secure the knot with a dab of glue (or clear nail polish - this dries quicker, and comes with its own brush).

Using a pair of long nosed pliers, gently squeeze the bead tip closed over the bead, then bend the metal arm down over the cap to form a loop. Place a jump ring or slip ring in the loop, and attach your other findings.

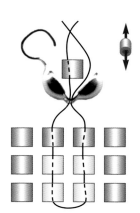

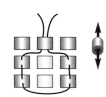

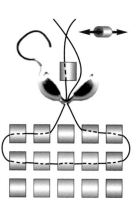

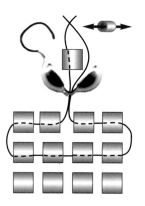

JUMP RINGS are split circles of wire used for connecting the metal findings together. Bend the jump ring sideways rather than opening it out, otherwise it will lose its shape. We mainly use 3mm and 5mm jump rings on most items.

SPRINGRING CLASPS are available in a range of sizes. Pictured left with ring and tag.

> **STERLING SILVER AND 9K GOLD FINDINGS ARE ALSO AVAILABLE FOR THOSE SPECIAL PIECES.**

BARREL CLASPS can be awkward to close on a bracelet singlehanded.

PARROT/LOBSTER CLASPS & RING are easy to close.

RING & TOGGLE are my favourite closure and there are many different styles and sizes.

SPECTACLE HOLDERS are available in black and white.

SHEPHERD HOOKS and other styles of earring findings are inexpensive and easy to find.

ALWAYS *use a new length of thread to attach your bead tip. Sometimes when closing a bead tip, the bead crushes and the thread is cut. It is easier to replace a new length of thread than unpick and then redo part of your beading. You also only really get one chance at bending the arm of a base metal bead tip, otherwise it can snap off, so take care. To be safe, I like to bend the arm before attaching it to the beading.*

You can use charted cross stitch designs for beading in square stitch or on a loom providing there are no fractional stitches used in the design and that the design is not dependant upon back stitch to define the different coloured areas.

You must also bear in mind that there will be a little distortion in the design as beads are not always the same width x height.

PROPORTIONS

When using 11/0 Delica beads with square stitch you must also bear in mind that threading up **7 BEADS AND WORKING 6 ROWS = 1CM** (*APPROX*).

Therefore to work a near perfect square in Delica's you would have to work within these proportions.

This is one of the reasons we put a beaded arrow beside our charts is so you can thread up your first row of beads and work the chart in the same direction we did, thus ensuring you get the correct proportions in your beading.

As our charts are drawn on a computer, we have the advantage of making a computer simulation to show us which is the best way to work the design.

THE PAPILIONIDAE BUTTERFLY FROM CS&B ISSUE 46 is a perfect example of this.

The arrows indicate the direction of the hole in the bead.

Turning the chart sideways will give you a taller, thinner design. Working the design as shown on the page and facing the right way, will give a shorter, rounder shape.

Both types of proportion can be used to advantage when beading as you may prefer a wider or narrower brooch or bag for example.

Left: Worked in cross stitch on 18 count vinyl weave. The proportion is correct

Right: Worked in square stitch using Delica 11/0 Japanese Cylinder Beads and Black Nymo D thread.

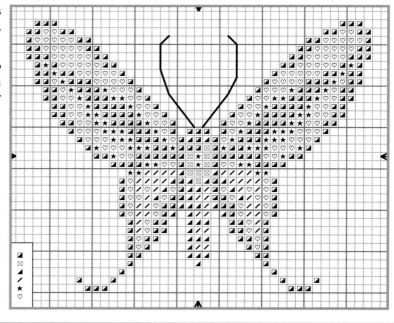

Bottom left: Worked in square stitch using Delica 11/0 Japanese Cylinder Beads and Grey Nymo D thread.

34 gauge wire was used for the feelers on the beaded butterflies.

Papilionidae

Stitch Count 41 wide x 33 high

ANCHOR	DBR		COLOUR KEY	QTY
403	◪	10	Black	267
236	⊠	631	Grey	10
306	◢	61	Dark Yellow	35
297	✎	42	Medium Yellow	45
244	★	916	Dark Green	71
241	♡	237	Medium Green	165

When beading a picture from a charted design, you will often have to chose your own beads to work it in. Jill Oxton's Cross Stitch & Beading will put in a bead colour key if we have worked the design, or a section of the design in beads, or know the colours will work for that design.

Beads can do strange things colourwise. What you think will be a light colour can quite often be very dark in relation to the other beads used around it.

The white violet on page 56 is a perfect example of this. Originally I chose three shades of "white" beads and started to work them in what I thought was the correct order by eye, but when stitched together, I had to reverse the order of the coloured beads as shown on the table below.

	CHOSE	USED
DARK WHITE	209	231
MEDIUM WHITE	351	209
LIGHT WHITE	231	251

The colour values have to step up and down quite a lot to be noticeable and the different finishes on beads also affect the colour values. The colour thread used can also affect the colour value too.

The easiest bead colours to work with are the matt finished beads as you do not have to take into account the reflections of the beads.

It takes a long time to build up a reliable colour palette for beading and if you have a nice colour run of beads (ie from dark to light in one colour), make sure you write them down for later use.

When working out your bead colour runs, make test swatches using the thread colour you intend to stitch them with. This will save many hours of frustration while working the project. They do not need to be large, mine are five beads wide by two rows of each colour I want to use, working from dark to light.

I stick all of my test swatches onto the back of old business cards, writing down the bead numbers, thread colour used and any other information I feel is relevant and file them in my bead box.

When beading a new design I start by choosing colours I have already used and know work well together and then add to them if necessary.

I aim to get a colour run of four beads and if the chart has five or more colours I will merge some of the colours together and use the same bead colour for this. As a general rule I will not merge the darkest and lightest colours, but will chose the middle colours to merge together.

WESTHIGHLAND TERRIER from CS&B ISSUE 57

cross stitched

Above and below are beaded using square stitch.

Note how the colour, shading and proportion can change from cross stitch to square stitch. But, each has its own appeal.

PIED HERON from CS&B ISSUE 50

cross stitched

We find that 11/0 Japanese Cylinder Beads and 11/0 Japanese Seed Beads sit best on 14 count fabrics such as 14ct Aida, 14ct Vinyl Weave, 14ct Perforated Plastic, 14ct Perforated Paper and 28 tpi *(threads per inch)* linen stitched over two threads of the fabric.

WE ALSO USE A SIZE 26 TO 28 TAPESTRY NEEDLE when stitching beads onto fabric, depending on the beads used.

WHEN USING BEADS WITH CROSS STITCH, we use both the stranded cotton and the bead for that relevant colour and find that this brings out the colour in the bead and can subtly alter the bead colour, particularly when using transparent beads.

IF WORKING AREAS OF BEADS AND AREAS OF CROSS STITCH TOGETHER *(ie stitching a flower in beads and the leaves in cross stitch)* we sew our beads onto the fabric using a half cross stitch or continental stitch (diagonal stitches), this way the beading butts up correctly with the cross stitch and doesn't leave a gap.

IF USING ALL BEADS FOR A DESIGN, the beads can be sewn onto the fabric using a horizontal, vertical or diagonal stitch and if the beads are not transparent they can be stitched using Nymo D thread in a colour that matches the colour of the fabric used.

IF BEADS ARE USED RANDOMLY THROUGHOUT THE DESIGN, we stitch them onto the fabric using a full cross stitch and match the thread to the fabric colour so that when the thread is carried across the fabric, it doesn't show through. If the beads are separated by more than ten stitches (ie, stars in the sky), after the full cross stitch has been worked through the bead, tie the tails of the thread together on the back of the fabric.

ROSE SPECTACLE CASES FROM CS&B ISSUE 48.

Left: The design was worked in cross stitch with pearl beads stitched on to the border using a half cross stitch.

Right: The design was worked in beads stitched on vertically using stranded cotton.

Above: The pink rose was worked in stranded cotton and beads using a half cross stitch and the leaves were worked in stranded cotton.

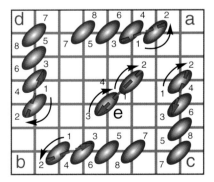

CONTINENTAL STITCH

a   Worked from right to left.
b   Worked from left to right.
c   Worked from top to bottom.
d   Worked from bottom to top

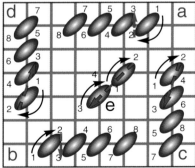

HALF CROSS STITCH

a   Worked from right to left.
b   Worked from left to right.
c   Worked from top to bottom.
d   Worked from bottom to top

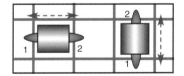

STITCHING A BEAD HORIZONTALLY OR VERTICALLY

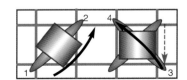

STITCHING A BEAD USING A FULL CROSS STITCH

Index of Stitches

Bibliography

Hawley, Anne, Spiral Rope, Hillsinger Fine Hand Beadwork.http://rogue.northwest.com/~ahawley/classroom.html>

Wilcox Wells, Carol, *Creative Bead Weaving, A contemporary guide to classic off-loom stitches,* Lark Books, North Carolina 1996 , ISBN 1-57990-080-1

Raven Willey, S, Peterburg Chain, <http://howlingrabbit.com/Projects/PbrgChain/PChain.html>

<http://beadwork.about.com/library

Contributors

ERIKA BANNA, based in Melbourne, Australia is a sales representative and beading demonstrator for the Australian distributor of Delica beads. The bracelets she designed were pounced upon and wheedled out of her when I saw them on the demonstration table. Erika is always asking me to sample her cooking, but unfortunately due to time restrictions and distance I haven't been able to yet.

MARGARET LEYLAND, located in Perth, Australia is a bead artist, cloth doll designer and teacher. Margaret introduced me to brick stitch for which I am grateful and I don't know if she cooks.

MARY MOTT, located in Adelaide South Australia, has been designing needlework for many years. Mary bakes me a Christmas cake every year.

DI NOYCE located in Adelaide South Australia, has been designing needlework for over twelve years. Di's work appears in Jill Oxton's Cross Stitch & Beading and without Di we wouldn't be where we are today. Di also paints, draws, dress makes and is an excellent cook.

GWENDOLYN OXTON located in Adelaide, South Australia, is the "sweet young thing" in our office, handling enquiries and orders. To my relief, although she didn't take to needlework, she loves beading. Gwendolyn doesn't know how to cook.

JILL OXTON located in Adelaide, South Australia, has been designing charted designs for over twenty years and is the publisher and editor of Jill Oxton's Cross Stitch & Beading. Jill avoids cooking where ever possible.

Above, Cheetah worked in Miyuki Delica 11/0 Japanese Cylinder Beads, from CS&B Issue 56